# TIBETAN FOOTHOLD

By the same author

FULL TILT
*Ireland to India with a Bicycle*

THE WAITING LAND
*A Spell in Nepal*

# Tibetan Foothold

Dervla Murphy

JOHN MURRAY

© DERVLA MURPHY 1966

*First published June 1966*
*Reprinted October 1966*
*Reprinted March 1968*

*Printed in Great Britain for*
*John Murray, Albemarle Street, London*
*by Butler & Tanner Ltd, Frome*
*and London*

7195 0989 0

6. 6. G P

This book is dedicated
to the
Tibetan Refugees

# Contents

# Illustrations

# *Foreword*

When I first became involved with Tibetan refugees—in July 1963—I knew no more about Tibet and her people than does the average European newspaper reader. The flight of the Dalai Lama in 1959 and China's final annexation of Tibet were vividly remembered, but to me the consequent exodus of refugees to India was just one more facet of our contemporary tragedy. So, for the benefit of those who may be equally vague on this subject, here is a general outline of the background to Tibetan affairs.

As soon as one attempts to clarify the history of Tibet's relations with China one is up against problems that refuse to be resolved in Western political terms. Doubts about whether a country is or is not an independent state may seem ridiculous to us now; yet even a century ago things were not so relentlessly organized, especially in Central Asia, and for this reason well-meaning efforts to make a water-tight case for Tibetan independence, *as we understand the term*, strike a slightly disingenuous note. Hugh Richardson writes: 'The Tibetans are admittedly by race, language, culture and religion a separate entity'—but this is not quite the point. One might say the same of the Gilgitis, for example, or of the inhabitants of other remote areas, yet these peoples do not necessarily claim political independence because of their separateness. The Tibetan question was virtually a matter of honour, requiring for its solution the application of humanity and common sense, rather than legalistic argument, and it is this fact which now moves so many people to sympathize with Tibet in a special way.

Recorded Tibetan history begins about A.D. 625 when Srongtsen Gam-po became king of Tibet and encouraged Nepalese Buddhist preachers to replace the old animistic Bön religion. In 763 the Tibetans captured Ch'ang-an, the Chinese capital, and in 821 a treaty, carved on a stone pillar which may still be seen at Lhasa, fixed the Tibetan–Chinese frontier near the present boundary of the Chinese province of Shensi. An anti-

Buddhist movement followed the accession of King Lang Darma (c. 838) and after his assassination in 842 the kingdom disintegrated into a number of minor monastic and lay principalities. Then came two hundred years of widespread reversion to the old religion, before the advent of the famous Bengali saint, Pandit Atisha, who revived Buddhism among the masses of the Tibetans.

In 1207 Tibet submitted to Chingis Khan, and in 1244 the Abbot of Sakya Monastery was made Viceroy of Tibet on behalf of the Mongols. This period of Mongol suzerainty lasted until 1368, when the Mongol Yuan dynasty of China, established by Kublai Khan, was deposed by the founders of the Ming dynasty and Tibet regained complete independence.

In 1578 the Lama Sonam Gyatso was given the title of Dalai Lama by the Mongol leader, Alton Khan, and in 1642 another Mongol leader, Gusri Khan, invaded Tibet, deposing the King and establishing the Fifth Dalai Lama, Ngawang Lobsang Gyatso, as ruler. Two years later the Manchu Ch'ing dynasty succeeded the Ming dynasty in China.

The next Mongol invasion of Tibet came in 1717, when Lhasa was seized, and three years later the Emperor Kiang Hsi sent an army to drive the Mongols out of Tibet and establish Imperial supervision over the Tibetan Government. These objectives achieved, the Chinese troops withdrew from Lhasa in 1723, but were back again in 1728, when civil war made the Emperor fear another Mongol invasion of the disunited country. On the restoration of peace the Tibetan Government was reorganized and Imperial representatives, known as Ambans, were posted to Lhasa and given a small military escort of Manchus. Twelve years later Sonam Topgye of Phola, who had been chief minister since the end of the civil war, was entitled King of Tibet. This ten-year reign was Tibet's last monarchical period, and when Phola's death in 1750 led to more unrest in Lhasa China again intervened and the Seventh Dalai Lama, Kesang Gyatso, was given the authority of supreme ruler.

China's next intervention in Tibetan affairs came in 1791, when a Nepalese invasion was repelled by Chinese troops. Again, in 1855, war broke out between Tibet and Nepal, but this time China did not come to the assistance of Tibet and the curious relationship which had existed between these two countries since 1720 was seen to be changing. This relationship had always been an informal and basically friendly arrangement, with Tibet accepting the nominal overlordship of the Emperor on the understanding that China would give military protection whenever the country or its religion was threatened. But until 1910 Tibetan administration was largely under Tibetan control, though it is difficult to assess what degree of influence the Ambans may have exerted from time to time.

The vagueness surrounding Tibet's status at the end of the last century is revealed by British actions at the time. It was initially impossible to determine who was actually in authority over the country, but when the Chinese failed to implement those treaties concerning Tibet which had been signed by their Imperial Government and the British Government, Britain decided to negotiate with Tibet as an independent state, while simultaneously attempting to respect the historic, if ill-defined links between that country and China.

During the first decade of this century the situation remained confused. In 1904 Britain, fearing a Russian invasion of her Indian Empire, invaded Tibet, occupied Lhasa and caused the flight of the Thirteenth Dalai Lama to China and Mongolia. An Anglo-Tibetan treaty was then signed, without reference to China; but two years later the Anglo-Chinese Convention gained Chinese agreement to this treaty, which Britain and China proceeded to modify, without reference to Tibet. These odd diplomatic manœuvres were followed, in 1908, by Chinese aggression on the eastern borders of Tibet and, in 1910, China staged its first invasion of Tibet for the purpose of incorporating that country into the Empire. This cleared the air considerably because the Dalai Lama, having taken refuge in India, vigorously repudiated the ancient tacit agreement between the two countries and pronounced Tibet to be an independent state. Two years later the overthrow of the Manchu dynasty enabled Tibet to free herself, and in January 1913 His Holiness returned to Lhasa.

Nine months later representatives of the Tibetan, Chinese and British Governments met at Simla on an equal footing. The British aim in organizing this conference was to achieve a

stable and clear-cut relationship between China and Tibet, but
the outcome—not altogether surprisingly—merely reclouded
the issue.

At first Tibet reluctantly agreed to forgo a part of its newly
proclaimed independence by acknowledging the suzerainty of
China, provided that China guaranteed the autonomy of Tibet
and agreed on a common frontier. But though the Chinese had
initialled the draft convention they refused to give it a full
signature so, when the British and Tibetan Governments
finally signed, they declared the Convention to be valid only
between themselves. The chief benefit thus withheld from
China was recognition of a strictly limited Chinese suzerainty
over Tibet, and from 1914 to 1947 the British Government
treated Tibet as an independent state.

During this period Tibet also acted as an independent state.
Her troops pushed the Chinese army east of the Yangtse in 1918
and in 1919, 1930, 1934 and 1940 she rejected China's attempts
to establish her claims to suzerainty. During the Second World
War both the Chinese and British Governments exerted pressure to have a free passage through Tibet for war-supplies to
China, but Tibet insisted on remaining neutral, just as Ireland
did when Sir Winston Churchill sought the use of Irish ports
in 1940. In 1948 a Tibetan Mission, with Tibetan passports,
visited Britain and America, and in July 1949, the Tibetan
Government expelled the Chinese Nationalist Mission from
Lhasa, two months before the Communist Government took
over in Peking.

The Indian Government recognized the new Chinese régime
in January 1950, but when the Communists announced that
they intended to 'liberate' Tibet Pandit Nehru replied, 'Liberate from whom?' On 7 October 1950 the Chinese began their
'liberation', and when the Indian Government protested the
reply was that 'Tibet is part of China'. Exactly a month later
the Tibetan Government appealed to the United Nations, but a
discussion on their appeal was postponed and their request for a
Commission of Enquiry was ignored. Then, on 23 May 1951,
Tibet was forced to capitulate to the might of China and the
'Seventeen Point Agreement' was signed in Peking.

Fourteen months later the Chinese set up their military and

civil headquarters at Lhasa, and in September 1952 their troops began to occupy strategic points throughout Tibet. It was at this time also that they installed their 'stooge' in the Panchen Lama's See of Shigatse. (After the Sixth Panchen Lama's quarrel with the Thirteenth Dalai Lama in 1923 he left for China, and died there in 1937. His successor, appointed by the Chinese Nationalist Government in 1949, was not acceptable to the Tibetans on religious grounds.)

In 1956 the people of the Amdo and Kham regions rebelled against the Chinese and by 1958 guerrilla warfare had spread to the Lhasa area. Chinese atrocities in Tibet had been steadily increasing and, though it was manifestly impossible for this tiny nation to repel China, it was inspired by the courage of despair to fight such oppression as best it could. The International Commission of Jurists, whose report *Tibet and the Chinese Peoples' Republic* was published from Geneva in July 1960, found unanimously that the Chinese in Tibet had been guilty of genocide.

On 10 March 1959 a special session of the National Assembly of Tibet met at Lhasa and denounced the 'Seventeen Point Agreement', many of whose articles had been contravened by the Chinese. It also reaffirmed—rather pathetically—Tibet's right to independence. During the following week tension increased daily in Lhasa and on 17 March the Dalai Lama fled to India and the Lhasa uprising began. Eleven days later the Chinese replaced the Tibetan Government by a military dictatorship.

Now the world at last became aware of Tibet's tragedy and, in October 1959, the General Assembly of the United Nations debated the question and passed, by 46 votes to 9 (with 26 abstentions), a kindly but ineffectual resolution demanding respect for human rights in Tibet. This resolution was sponsored by Malaya and Ireland and it makes me proud to quote from Hugh Richardson's pamphlet on the subject. He writes:

The Resolution was proposed with ability and feeling by Dato Nik Kamil, of the Federation of Malaya; but the most memorable figure in the discussions was Mr Frank Aiken of Ireland, who made a deep impression both in the Steering

Committee and in the General Assembly by the dignity, humanity and sincere conviction with which he spoke. The Tibetans should be grateful to him and to the whole Irish delegation for the spirit and energy they devoted to studying the facts and making them known.

Two of the countries which might have been expected to give Tibet full support—Britain and India—were among those who abstained. Though Britain had treated Tibet as an independent state since 1914 her delegate, Sir Pierson Dixon, now said that his Government 'did not take up a final or definite position on the matter'. To Tibet's many friends in Britain this giving the benefit of the doubt to the bully in the case came as a bitter disappointment and was a grim illustration of the dominance of expediency over honour in political circles.

India's betrayal of Tibet in the Assembly was less unexpected because the Indian Government had already censured the Dalai Lama for appealing to the United Nations. Yet in 1947 this same Government had inherited Britain's attitude to Tibet and, until the Sino-Indian agreement of 1954, had acted upon the assumption that Tibet was an independent nation. India and Britain were the two countries who best knew the truth about Tibet, but Mr Krishna Menon's speech showed either inexcusable ignorance or deliberate malice. He said that 'India inherited the British position in Tibet in 1947—that is to say, that Tibet was under Chinese suzerainty'. This blatant misrepresentation of the facts, which could—and should—have been contradicted by Sir Pierson, was allowed to confuse the issue further, and the British delegate continued to play China's game by proposing that, 'as full discussions had taken place, a resolution was not really necessary'. This idea was given the reception it deserved.

In its 1960 report the International Commission of Jurists found that 'Tibet demonstrated from 1913 to 1950 the conditions of statehood as generally accepted under International Law'. The Commission did not find it necessary to declare whether Tibet's independence was *de jure* or *de facto*, but no disinterested student of the case could disagree with their verdict. However, it came too late to affect the situation materially;

in 1950, when Tibet first appealed to the United Nations, no government—except, curiously, that of El Salvador—had any knowledge of Tibet's status.

Undeniably Tibet's deliberate isolationism helped to make it convenient for the free world to ignore the Chinese threat. She has never wished to project a flattering image of herself onto the world-screen nor to 'keep up with the Joneses' in material advance. Foreigners and their ideas were severely discouraged from entering Tibet, no diplomatic missions were maintained abroad and the country did not even belong to the World Postal Union. With characteristic simplicity she believed that by minding her own business and doing no harm to anyone she could escape involvement in the nasty complexities of the modern world—though history should have taught her that no country can stand alone.

Numerically the Tibetan refugee problem is a minor one. It is impossible to give accurate figures, but the most reliable estimate says that there are 4,000 Tibetan refugees in Bhutan, 5,000 in Sikkim, 7,000 in Nepal and 60,000 in India. This gives a total of only 76,000, yet the singularity of Tibetan traditions complicates the situation out of all proportion to the numbers involved; for these refugees resettlement means adjusting not only to an alien country but to an alien century, in which current values are sadly antipathetic to the Tibetan way.

# Introduction to Tibland

To arrive in Delhi during the early part of July constitutes gross mismanagement of an itinerary—especially if one arrives by bicycle. My first week in the capital was spent recovering from heat-stroke; then, putting aside all thoughts of cycling during the months ahead, I began to make tentative enquiries about the possibility of doing some voluntary social work until November's coolness came to the rescue and I could start cycling again.

The enquiries were tentative because my accomplishments were so few. I could not drive a car, teach, nurse, type, keep accounts or speak any language but English; in fact my only discernible skill was long-distance cycling, which seemed totally irrelevant. Yet, like Barkis, I was willin', and chance did the rest.

I had an introduction to Mrs Llewellen, sister of Mr Beck whom I had met at the British Embassy in Kabul, and when I called on her one evening she said that I simply must meet Mrs Bland, who lived near by and came from Ireland. Within half an hour I had met Mrs Bland, who in turn said that I simply must meet Mrs Buxton, an Englishwoman who knew a great deal about India's social problems.

This suggestion was very welcome as I already felt myself becoming drugged by the oddly soporific atmosphere of New Delhi's foreign colony. Even a week spent in such a cosmopolitan pocket of luxury tends to blunt one's perception of the realities of Indian life, and contact with someone like Mrs Buxton seemed an ideal escape route. The difficulty was that a slight aura of mystery surrounded this Mrs Buxton and no one knew her whereabouts. She did not, I gathered, belong to the Western social bloc in Delhi, nor had she any fixed address; but she regularly visited the Cheshire Home at Kalkaji—on the famous Ridge immortalized during the uprising of 1857—and on 17 July I went there in search of her, leaving my friend's house on Janpath at 5.30 in the morning to avoid that heat which by 8 a.m. would be torturing the city. Yet despite this precaution I arrived at Kalkaji saturated with sweat, after an easy eight-mile cycle.

Over breakfast with Mrs Davies, the Anglo-Indian matron, I explained my problem and she promised to do her best to contact the elusive Mrs Buxton. The rest of the morning I spent talking to the patients; it was heartening to see at least a score of India's destitute being so well cared for—but depressing to think of all the millions who need similar care and can't have it. For a citizen of a tiny country like Ireland it takes time to get adjusted to the immensity of every Indian problem.

The Home overlooks an undulating landscape, now shrivelled to dull dust. While waiting for lunch I sat on a mud roof in the shade of a peepul tree and looked down on the stagnant, scummy waters of a little lake into which emaciated buffaloes were being driven for their daily splash. Near them an equally emaciated Hindu was vigorously washing himself, standing waist-deep a yard out from the shore and pushing the green scum aside before plunging his head under water. Above, the sky was like a reflection of the landscape, colourless with heat, and kites and vultures wheeled slowly round, ever vigilant for carrion. Below, in the compound, two women were quarrelling shrilly in Hindi and their irritation communicated itself ridiculously to me. Clouds of flies buzzed and tickled; the hot, greasy odours of curry and ghee, rising from the kitchen, killed any flicker of appetite I might have felt. Beside me sat a lugubrious Hindu youth, telling me of his domestic troubles in singsong Indian English: his mother had fought so incessantly with his bride of a year ago that the girl had returned to her parents and he had not yet seen his all-important first-born son, now a fortnight old. I listened to the sad, unoriginal story with an odd lack of sympathy. By midday, in such weather, a deadly apathy —physical, mental and emotional—takes possession of me, so that I can register nothing but the unsavoury impact which India makes simultaneously on all the senses.

After a token lunch I fell fast asleep in Mrs Davies's sitting-room, and when I was awakened at 2 p.m. by a hand on my shoulder I looked up dopily to see someone sitting beside me—it was Mrs Buxton.

Before we had been talking for five minutes I could see that
she was one of those people who are born with a flair for living
happily outside the framework of tiresome conventions, and
neither of us wasted any time. I explained my ambition, listing
all the ways in which I could not possibly be of the slightest
assistance to anyone—but adding that I did have an infinite
capacity for roughing it. As I talked, I was aware of being very
thoroughly sized up; Jill Buxton's vague and amiable manner
does not entirely camouflage her shrewdness.

When I had finished she asked, 'Would you like to work with
Tibetan refugees?' Then she went on to outline graphically the
appalling conditions prevailing in most of the refugee camps. It
soon became clear that in such surroundings something worthwhile could be achieved by any able-bodied person who was
willing to co-operate with the medical staff, and I replied un-
hesitatingly that I would love to work for Tibetans.

When we left the Home I was introduced to Arabella, the
Land-Rover in which Jill had driven to India two years previously. Like myself, she had had no fixed plans on arriving,
but Mrs Freda Bedi, the English-born principal of the Young
Lama's School at Dalhousie, had put her in touch with the
Tibetan problem—in which she has been deeply involved ever
since.

On meeting Arabella I saw why no one knew Jill Buxton's
address: she lives in Arabella, cooking on a primus-stove and
sleeping on the front seats, to the horror of all those who consider it both dangerous and unseemly for a Memsahib to behave
in this fashion.

In turn I introduced Jill to Rozinante, the long-suffering
bicycle which had taken me from Ireland to India; then Roz
was loaded into Arabella and we drove back to Delhi, through
blistering heat which almost annihilated me but left Jill cheerfully unaffected.

During the following week I spent most of my time getting
to know the various international relief agencies which help the
Tibetans, meeting members of the Delhi Tibetan colony and
learning a lot from Jill about the many awkward angles of the
refugee problem.

It was eventually decided that I should go to the transit

camp-cum-school at Kangra, where 300 children were living in unbelievably squalid conditions. As Jill was now planning one of her tours of the camps we arranged to leave Delhi together on 22 July, by which date she hoped to have collected a supply of clothing, tinned foods and medicines. But in the East things rarely happen at the appointed time and the 22nd became the 23rd, and then the 24th, before we were ready to start.

The parched Punjab landscape is not very inspiring immediately before the monsoon, yet it was good to be out in the country again, after sixteen days in a city. For 150 miles Jill kept Arabella to the straight, flat Grand Trunk Road along which I had cycled by moonlight on my way from Pakistan to Delhi; and then, a few miles beyond Ambala, we turned north towards the hills.

Twenty miles further on the road began to climb steeply; the landscape became suddenly green and rain-washed, the air was dust-free and the insidious stench of the plains—which permeates even the best-run homes—was replaced by the strong tang of resin. As Arabella swung effortlessly around countless sharp bends my spirits rose perceptibly with the increasing coolness of every mile.

On each side the mountains were dense with trees, shrubs and ferns, and occasionally a clear stream sparkled across the road. This fertility would be taken for granted at home but now I looked at it with something akin to a sense of reverence. We spent the night at Kasauli, a little hill-station perched cheekily on a ridge 6,400 feet above sea-level. By day the view from here is splendid enough, but by night it is quite magical, for then the lights of Simla, forty miles away, can be seen twinkling in their thousands on the crest of another mountain.

At Kasauli Service Civil International runs a nursery for about fifty Tibetan refugees under the age of seven. Two British International Voluntary Service workers—David Williams and Robert Bell—had done a great deal to improve the building during the previous six months and I reflected that such projects show the brighter side of our so-often-condemned age. The youth of earlier generations left home and travelled

the world usually for gain of some sort, however ingeniously
their motives may have been wrapped in pious phrases; but now
a number of highly qualified young people, impatient of the
meaningless luxury of their own society, choose to work with
the 'have-nots' on a daily maintenance allowance of one and
sixpence.

The other helpers were an elderly Indian 'housefather', a
thirty-year-old Tibetan and a young Japanese nurse. All these
people, of widely different backgrounds, were co-operating
generously to make this effort a success, and the homely atmosphere more than made up for a frugal standard of living,
shared alike by the children and the volunteers.

When Jill and I arrived at the entrance to the nursery playground our appearance caused a demonstration that astonished
me. From every direction the children came running towards
us, with outstretched arms, greeting us as though we were long-
lost friends. All they wanted was to be picked up and cuddled,
and their unselfconscious revelation of this basic need completely disarmed me. In his book *Tibetan Marches*, Dr André
Migot writes:* 'As for Tibetan children, they can only be
described as adorable. . . .' Remembering this, while these
toddlers hugged my legs and climbed all over me, I saw
exactly what he meant. Many of them were in pretty poor
shape, suffering from scabies and general malnutrition, yet
they glowed with good humour; and later, at the evening dispensary session, I observed that Tibetan gaiety was equalled by
Tibetan docility. Diminutive four-year-olds stoically swallowed
gigantic sulpha tablets without a murmur and one five-year-old
boy stood unflinchingly, his head laid on the nurse's lap, while
she dressed an agonizing ear-abscess.

After the children had chanted their night prayers and been
put to bed by the four Tibetan ayahs, Jill and I dined with the
volunteers. During the meal we discussed the Indian Army's
recent threat to requisition the Nursery building; obviously
someone had blundered badly by not ensuring, before invest-
ing precious time and money, that no such threat could be
made. I heard later that, through the kindness of the Area
Commanding Officer, S.C.I. were allowed to retain the house;

* *Tibetan Marches*, Hart-Davis, 1955.

but this was my first experience of the inefficiency too often connected with aid to the Tibetans. Many individuals and organizations are helping the refugees, yet the lack of co-ordination—either through insufficient knowledge of the over-all picture or because of petty jealousies between rival organizations—sadly diminishes the sum total of good achieved.

Looking back on my initiation into the refugee world such a short time ago it is strange to remember my innocent assumption that everyone involved in this type of work puts refugees first; the disillusionment was extreme when it became obvious to me that a large minority put themselves or their organizations first and remain coolly detached from refugees as human beings. This does not, of course, apply to the full-time field-workers, almost all of whom are genuinely concerned and who have little interest in the machinations of the powers-that-be in London, Delhi or New York. These machinations are by no means confined to Tibetan relief work, but recently several experienced people have remarked to me that the Tibetans do seem to bring out the worst in relief agencies—possibly because this race has 'something special' and stimulates extra possessiveness. Admittedly such criticisms leave one open to charges of 'crankiness'; people argue that 'human nature being what it is one can't expect anything else', and no doubt this is partly true. Yet in Big Business human nature is not allowed to impede efficiency so drastically and it seems only reasonable to aim at a similar discipline in the administration of refugee aid.

Another of the basic problems of this situation arises from the cultural gulf between Western helpers and an Eastern people; what looks like an excellent scheme to an American or European may well have a disastrous effect on a group of Tibetans. However, this difficulty should diminish in time if each side makes the necessary effort to understand the other's point of view.

On the following afternoon Jill and I arrived in Simla. Like the Red Fort in Old Delhi, Simla is one of India's ghost-haunts—though instead of the formidable elegance of the Fort one sees here a monument to the Victorian penchant for ugliness on a grand scale. The skill with which a large town was built on such vertical slopes gives the place a certain interest and charm, but from a visitor's point of view Simla's fall from glory is as yet too recent for it to seem anything more than an embarrassing example of the fragility of empires.

One hundred and thirty years ago this 7,300-foot mountain was as inaccessible and deserted as its neighbouring peaks. Then an enterprising army lieutenant built himself a bungalow near the summit and within a few years the mountain-top had been transformed by the magic wand of wealth and power into a centre of imperial opulence. Here, until 1947, the British lived during the hot season in their own little world, comfortably cushioned on the knowledge that they were indispensable to India, yet remaining as remote from the fundamental realities of Indian life as Simla is from the sweat and dust of the plains. Then, less than a century after Simla's creation, there was no more Empire. Overnight, the town became an ill-at-ease holiday resort for Indians, who now stroll along those streets which not long ago were forbidden to their race. Yet the spirit of Simla remains obstinately British, just as the spirit of the Red Fort remains Moghul, and this must indeed be flattering to the Indians who, looking at these reminders of past conquests, can see that however omnipotent the invaders may once have been, they all finally succumbed to the implacable vastness of India.

The Save the Children Fund runs two Tibetan Homes at Simla—'Stirling Castle', on Elysium Hill, and 'The Manor', on Summer Hill—each caring for about 150 children under the age of eight. At Chota Simla there is an Indian Government-run boarding-school for some 500 boys and girls, and to this establishment the children are transferred from the S.C.F. nurseries.

Our first stop in Simla was at 'Stirling Castle'. As Arabella ascended the perilously steep drive we overtook a group of neatly dressed, spotlessly clean children being shepherded home from their afternoon walk by two equally clean and neat Tibetan ayahs. The contrast with the ill-clad, unhealthy Kasauli toddlers was marked; yet these Simla children, though obviously contented and cheerful, were also noticeably more subdued and disciplined—no doubt along kind but firm Western lines. And soon I realized that this difference presented a microcosm of the whole Tibetan problem.

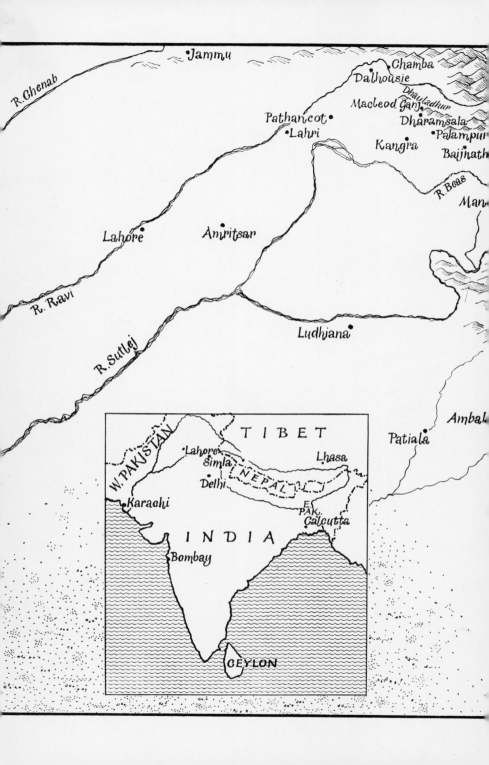

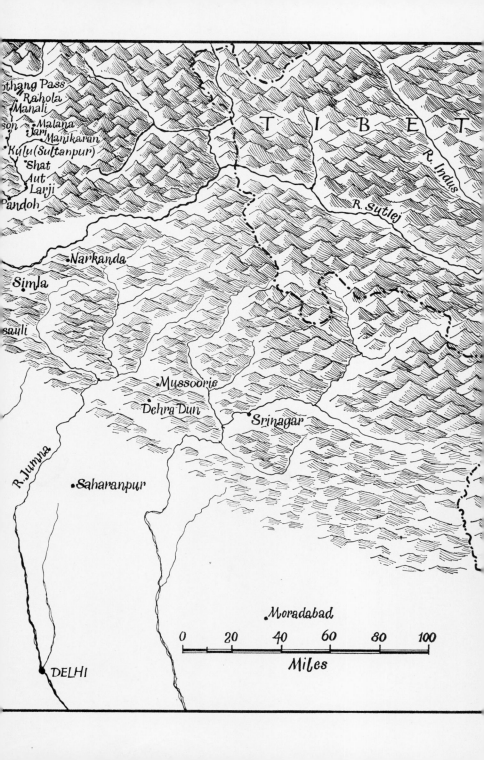

othang Pass
Rahola
Manali
son
Malana
Jari Manikaran
Kulu (Sultanpur)
Shat
Aut
Larji
Pandoh

TIBET

R. Indus

R. Sutlej

Narkanda

Simla

sauli

Mussoorie

Dehra Dun

Srinagar

R. Jumna

Saharanpur

Moradabad

0    20    40    60    80    100

Miles

DELHI

The kernel of the problem is the extent to which these refugees should be encouraged to conform to the world in which they now live—a question on which I soon found myself hopelessly split. My reason told me that Tibetans, as Tibetans, were doomed, while my instinct fiercely opposed every move which might hasten the process of absorbing them into any other culture. To live among these people is a lesson in the uses of courage, and the destruction of their unique way of life is one of the greatest tragedies of this century. However, it is now a *fait accompli* and, though one must sympathize with official Tibetan efforts to preserve their national integrity, fanaticism on this point seriously hinders the resettlement of the peasants.

For a few years after the establishment of the Tibetan Government-in-Exile its policy was based on the assumption that Tibet would soon be liberated and that then all her refugees could return home to live happily ever after in the changeless Tibetan way. Unfortunately this policy made it much more difficult to help the people to adjust to a new way of life and one hopes that the Tibetan Government's newly displayed realism on the subject will now spread as rapidly as possible among the people.

Many Westerners urge that the unusually adaptable Tibetans should be immediately integrated into other societies—a plan which has the virtues of simplicity and practicality. Yet it is basically defeatist and one would like to believe that with the co-operation of the Tibetan Government some compromise may be achieved between the conflicting policies of preserving Tibetan culture intact and abruptly abandoning it to pursue 'sensible' integration.

When Arabella stopped outside Stirling Castle a lean, bearded figure came leaping agilely down the slope, and a moment later we were introducing ourselves to Stuart Menteth, the newly appointed S.C.F. administrator for India. At once I mentally nick-named him 'Bertie Wooster' as his charm and phraseology were of the waffling and slightly archaic Wodehouse vintage; but I soon discovered that this façade concealed qualities which had already infused a great deal of badly needed common-sense into the administration of local S.C.F. projects. His wife, Pauline, who welcomed us into their little bungalow, was equally capable, being the sort of Englishwoman who tackles the most improbable tasks with an invincible mixture of guts, humour and compassion. Though lacking any previous experience of such work she managed to keep a complex situation tactfully under control and was immensely popular among the Tibetans.

For me the little tea-party which followed in the Menteth's bed-sittingroom was quite an historic occasion. We ate English-style cucumber sandwiches and Tibetan-style pastries, baked in the shape of miniature toast-racks, while the Menteths told us about the desperate situation at Dharamsala Nursery.

This camp, the largest of its kind in India, was opened in May 1960 by Mrs Tsiring Dolma, the elder sister of the Dalai Lama, soon after His Holiness moved from Mussoorie to Dharamsala. By June 1963 there were over 1,100 children in the camp, which had adequate accommodation for about 300, and at this point S.C.F. sent a fully trained nurse—Juliet Maskell, from Birmingham—to cope with the crisis as best she could. Not surprisingly, Juliet collapsed from overwork after six weeks, and was now a patient in Kangra Mission Hospital. The Menteths were in despair about this situation and by the time tea had been cleared away it was obvious that my destination would have to be Dharamsala instead of Kangra.


On the following morning Jill and I drove down to Chota Simla School, which introduced me to the squalor of refugee camp life. At that time the buildings were overcrowded, leaking and crawling with bed-bugs; inadequate sanitation made it impossible to control the spread of dysentery and worms, and the hungry children were clad in rags. However, after talking at some length to the Indian headmaster—who showed more imaginative sympathy for the Tibetans than do most of his race —I realized that this was not the worst of it. Housing, feeding and clothing are comparatively simple problems—and since that time conditions have improved enormously at Chota Simla —but no plan for the resettlement of untrained youngsters in an already overpopulated country has yet been suggested.

None of these children had any schooling in Tibet and now they are being taught a smattering of English, Hindi, arithmetic and geography—an educational policy which is both farcical and potentially destructive. As the sons and daughters of illiterate agriculturists and nomad herdspeople they have inherited a fine tradition of crop-cultivation and stock-breeding—skills to which Tibetans bring a high degree of natural intelligence. They have also inherited many other talents, such as weaving, dyeing, leather-work and metal-work, and it is generally recognized that Tibetans possess an exceptional sense of colour and design. Yet at the various schools these children are being taught the rudiments of subjects which bear no relation to their natural aptitudes. In Tibet 'book learning' was the speciality of Lamas and aristocrats, and its effect on the young refugees is obviously going to be a disastrous discontent with their lot and a contempt for the crafts at which their forefathers excelled.

At present, fortunately for the Tibetans, the Indian Government is building new military roads to the northern frontier and this gives employment to about eighteen thousand refugees of both sexes—an arrangement which also suits India, since at high altitudes one Tibetan can do the work of five Indians. Among these road-workers are hundreds of skilled craftsmen, who now spend their days breaking stones or shifting soil and who are the only remaining link with the artistic splendours of old Tibet. It seemed to me, when I first heard of this situation, that it should be within someone's power to assemble these craftsmen, provide them with the necessary materials, select the children most likely to profit from their teaching and let them go on from there. However, I soon discovered that nothing is ever as simple as it looks in what a friend of mine calls 'Tibland'—the world of Tibetan refugees, Indian Government officials and Western charity organizations. The disheartening thing is that one can never find out *why* a given project is not considered feasible. Several different reasons may come from several different directions, but the truth, as so often in India, remains forever hidden. If there were a shortage of funds this would not be so unbearable, but money worries are no longer a major problem in Tibland. The fate of Tibet left the governments of the world callously unmoved when their help was most needed, yet the plight of the refugees so stirred the sympathy of ordinary people everywhere that vast sums of money have been subscribed over the past six years. Now the principal needs are: (*a*) a pooling of resources by the Indian Government and the many organizations involved, (*b*) people of vision and integrity to administer this central fund and (*c*) a generous discarding of red tape by both Tibetan and Indian officials. The resettlement of the Tibetans bristles with complications—political, social and philosophical—and a satisfactory solution cannot possibly be found amidst the prevailing bureaucratic chaos.

On our way back to Stirling Castle we learned that the direct Simla–Dharamsala road was now impassable, as the monsoon had already broken in the hills, so Jill announced that we would have to return to the plains and follow the Grand Trunk Road westwards for another eighty miles. We left Simla late that evening and, after a glorious moonlit drive through the mountains, stopped again at Kasauli.

Soon after leaving the G. T. Road at Jullundur, on the following afternoon, the countryside again became beautiful in a quiet, green way. But soon the landscape grew wilder and rockier, as Arabella climbed smoothly into the hills that divide the Punjab Plain from the Kangra valley.

We camped after dark near the little town of Dehra, on a cliff high above the Beas river—which made a splendid silver swathe in the moonlight. Within an hour Jill was fast asleep in Arabella and I was almost asleep, wrapped in a blanket on the grass verge of the track. But the night was hot, though dewy, so I threw off the blanket—an action which the local mosquitoes interpreted as an invitation to supper. Having dissuaded them by applying the relevant cream I had just fallen asleep when I was loudly sniffed at by a deputation of astonished dogs, investigating the mystery of the foreign body; then, after their departure, the dew became so heavy that I had to resume my blanket and I spent the remainder of the night restlessly sweating within its shelter.

By 10 a.m. the following morning we were viewing from the south the long, east-to-west Kangra valley, with its tremendous northern backdrop of the Dhauladhur spur of the Himalayas. High on the side of one of these mountains, 4,000 feet above the valley floor, I was to live during the next four months. As it happened, this was the last of the sunshine before the monsoon broke—had we come a day later I would have had to wait five weeks to see the snowy ridges above Dharamsala.

Kangra town, overlooking the Ban Ganga torrent, is cobbled, hilly and smelly. Many of its streets are closed to motor-traffic so we walked to the Tibetan Boys' School, run by the Tibetan Ministry for Education, in the town centre. Passing through the violently coloured bazaar, where flies swarm in millions, I studied the pale-skinned, cheerful faces of the locals and realised that they were as different from the people 'down-country' as their valley is different from the plains. Most of them are semi-nomad herdspeople who take their flocks to high summer pastures in the Himalayas and, though there is little wealth in this valley, they are sturdy and contented. Kangra is only 2,000 feet above sea-level and is reputed to be one of the unhealthiest spots in India; it would be difficult to choose an area less suited to refugees from the 'Roof of the World'.

Approaching the school we heard the boys chanting lessons from the Buddhist scriptures, as they sat crossed-legged in tidy rows on the parched earth of the playground. Conditions here were much the same as at Chota Simla. This place was then being run by a Rimpoche, or Incarnate Lama, named Khantoul—a young man of twenty-five, dressed, most disappointingly, in slacks and a cotton shirt—who showed us round the dilapidated, rat-infested building. Then came the inevitable tea and biscuits in his tiny office, followed by a P.T. display for our entertainment. Wherever one encounters groups of Tibetan children in India P.T., for some mysterious reason, ranks high on the list of their accomplishments. So far as I know there is nothing in their national tradition to account for this phenomenon and the only explanation I have ever heard is that each child is regarded by the Tibetan authorities as a future member of Tibet's Liberation Army and that the P.T. cult is part of their military training.

From the boys' school we walked up hundreds of stone steps to the Canadian Mission Hospital. Here Dr Haslem—a remarkable woman who has been running this hospital for the past thirty years—told us that Juliet could return to Dharamsala on the following day, if she avoided overwork for another week. (It was, I noted, accepted that she would have to over-work once her convalescence had ended.) Then Juliet joined us; she looked pale and tired, but was obviously determined to per-suade all concerned that she was again in perfect health. When we had been introduced Jill explained that I was coming to Dharamsala to work under her. I had been slightly apprehen-sive about this moment, in view of my total ignorance of medicine, but Juliet's welcome at once reassured me.

During the next four months Juliet and I were to share the small S.C.F. bungalow which had just been built at the edge of the Nursery compound. It was clear from the start that we had absolutely nothing in common. I am incurably untidy; Juliet is miserable if any object strays a millimetre to right or left of its appointed place. I work until midnight but Juliet retires early. I fail to get on well with Indians and Juliet—who previously worked for eighteen months at Darjeeling and Delhi—is com-pletely at home with them. Even our attitudes to the Tibetans were opposed; Juliet regarded them as so many patients to be nursed back to health and affirmed that she saw no difference between English, Tibetans and Indians—except that the lament-ably uncivilized Tibetans needed lessons in hygiene rather more urgently than anyone else. I, on the other hand, had most un-professionally fallen in love with all my patients and to me the Tibetans represented what Fosco Maraini describes as 'Perhaps the only civilization of another age to have survived intact into our own time'.

At first sight it seemed lunatic to enclose two such dissimilar women in a confined space and expect them both to survive. And yet, miraculously, we never quarrelled. Juliet's patience and thoughtfulness were monumental. She tolerated the nause-ating clouds of cigarette smoke with which I filled our little bedroom and the piles of reference books and sheaves of manuscript that wandered all over our cramped floor space, apparently of their own volition. She never interrupted when I was writing and I soon acquired the knack of not hearing her transistor. Inevitably I felt the strain of never being alone, yet by the end of our four months together Juliet and I had developed a sincere mutual affection.

At the Kangra School for Tibetan girls, about two miles beyond the town, Jill and I were welcomed by a most engaging couple, who fed us more tea and biscuits before taking us to count the holes in the roof directly over their new supply of beds and blankets.

Then a group of the girls spontaneously decided to perform some of those extraordinary dances which were later to become so familiar. Observing the happiness of these youngsters I was astonished. Many had been forced to leave family and friends behind them when they escaped to India and some had certainly witnessed terrifying scenes of cruelty, as the Chinese tightened their grip on Tibet. I wondered then to what extent suspense, loneliness and the memory of past horrors still affected them emotionally. Later, at Dharamsala, I noticed that some of the adolescents, and a few adults too, were prone to sudden hysterical outbursts for trivial reasons. Yet on balance it appeared to me that the Tibetans' racial temperament and religious faith did enable them to overcome cheerfully the distresses of a refugee life.

That evening Jill and I camped between Kangra and Lower Dharamsala. On our left the narrow road was overhung by high cliffs of earth and rock, while on our right there was a two-hundred-foot drop to river level. Arabella had to be parked on the edge of the precipice to leave room for passing military traffic and at about 9 p.m. I curled up in my blanket just behind her. After the disturbed rest of the previous night I was soon asleep—but before long a passing peasant prodded me in the ribs and considerately pointed out that rockfalls on this stretch of the road normally landed precisely where we were sleeping. I in turn woke Jill and we blearily proceeded to what seemed a safer spot, but this time, just in case it wasn't, I settled down under Arabella's protection.

The next diversion came at 11 p.m., when an army officer returning to Upper Dharamsala mistook me for a dead body. Assured that I was nothing of the sort he remarked encouragingly that at the present rate of progress I soon would be and then proceeded on his way. After this I didn't go to sleep for some time—not because the officer's pessimistic prophecy had unnerved me, but because I am much addicted to thunderstorms, and a particularly impressive specimen was now taking place. There are few experiences more stirring than the arrogant reverberations of thunder in high mountains.

Soon after midnight the storm abated and I dozed off, to be re-awakened just after 3 a.m. by Jill shining a torch under Arabella and yelling: 'Are you all right?' Her voice was barely audible above the continuous crashing of thunder overhead and the rushing hiss of torrential train. I was about to reply sleepily, 'Yes, thank you', when I woke up enough to realize that I was very far from being all right. A young river was racing down the road and I was lying in inches of water. At that moment we heard a menacing bumping near by, as dislodged rocks rolled down the precipice. Jill exclaimed: 'For God's sake get out of that! We must move or the road will collapse under Arabella.' So off we went again, though visibility was almost nil and gigantic waterfalls were roaring off the cliffs onto the road. Above the din Jill shouted cheerfully: 'If anyone saw us now they'd say we were mad—and they'd be right!' Actually we were enjoying ourselves enormously and for me this was an unforgettable introduction to the annual drama of the breaking of the monsoon.

A few miles further on we came at last to a really safe spot. By now the water on the road was six inches deep so I squeezed into the back of Arabella—which was not dry, but slightly less wet than the road. Here, reclining on crates of Heinz Baby Food, I slept from 4 to 6 a.m.—when I was quite surprised to wake up of my own accord.


Dharamsala is divided into two sections—Lower Dharamsala, at 4,500 feet, and Upper Dharamsala, at 6,000 feet. Lower Dharamsala is the headquarters of Kangra District and, like many towns whose prosperity depended on the British, it now seems slightly sorry for itself. Upper Dharamsala, which was a popular hill-station before the earthquake of 1905 levelled most of the houses, is at present famous as a Tibetan enclave. Here are the Palace of His Holiness the Dalai Lama, the headquarters of the Tibetan Government-in-Exile and the training centre of the Tibetan Drama Party. These institutions, to-

gether with the Nursery for Tibetan Children and the hundreds
of Tibetan squatters who have occupied nearby hamlets, give
the whole area such a Tibetan flavour that within a week of
coming here I found it difficult to remember that I was still in
India.

It is possible to walk from Lower to Upper Dharamsala in
fifty minutes, using the old path which climbs through forests of
giant rhododendrons and deodars, at times becoming a stairway of rock; but by the new motor-road that swivels dizzily
around the mountains this is an eight-mile journey. When we
drove up on 29 July the violence of the monsoon was almost
frightening. Everywhere water forcefully had its way, making a
mockery of the apparent solidity of the hills as it ripped great
wounds in their flanks and uprooted their bushes.

One could smell the Nursery before it became visible through
this downpour. Up on our right the earth embankment of the
compound was covered with excrement, now being distilled by
the rain. Already this dominant stench had become for me one
of the hall-marks of a Tibetan camp—that and the ragged,
faded prayer flags which flutter indomitably wherever Tibetans
gather—but here at Dharamsala the stench was a classic of its
kind, with 1,100 contributors concentrated in one small area.

Jill drove carefully across the compound—a sea of sticky
mud—and then backed up to the S.C.F. bungalow. The strange
sight of a Land-Rover brought hundreds of excited children
from the shelter of those crowded rooms to which they are
confined twenty-four hours a day during the monsoon. Hungry,
dirty and covered in sores, they stood watching intently while
we unloaded the clothes, medicines and tinned foods which
would make life a little easier for some of them.

Chumba and Kesang helped us to unload. Chumba was the
camp cook, whose broad smile and kindly eyes were almost
warm and bright enough to dispel the rains; Kesang was
Juliet's young servant, who shared our bungalow, unrolling her
bedding each night on one of the hard, wooden Tibetan
couches. As Juliet pointed out, it was essential for a personal
servant to 'sleep in' if she were to be kept sufficiently lice-free to
look after our food and clothing. The other twenty ayahs on
the compound showed the traditional Tibetan distaste for

c

removing extraneous matter from the skin and were chronically lice-ridden. Most of them had no rooms of their own, and at nightfall one found them sleeping in corners, looking like so many rolled-up bundles. The few who were married, or living with the man of their choice, had 'homes' in tiny, airless rooms measuring about six feet square. Yet they were all good-tempered and seemingly happy on a wage of fifteen shillings a month, though they worked a seven-day week.

We were joined for lunch by Oliver Senn, a Swiss Red Cross doctor who had arrived at the camp only two weeks previously. Already, at twenty-seven, Oliver was almost a caricature of the absent-minded professor and I wasn't in the least surprised to discover, months later, that during his university career he had published a treatise on some impossibly abstruse branch of modern medicine. Tall, slim, slightly stooping, slightly bald and slightly near-sighted, Oliver spoke English fluently but quaintly and was given to blinking rapidly when brought up against the bewildering practicalities of life. To offset his prodigious erudition on a variety of subjects he had a child's capacity for enjoying the simplest pleasures. And when you met Oliver you also met Claudia, his fiancée, who at that time was doing her medical finals in Switzerland and who was by a long way Oliver's favourite topic of conversation.

Oliver lived in a damp, windowless cell behind the Dispensary—the sort of place in which no Englishman would keep a dog. Here he wrote official reports and did laboratory tests until the small hours of every morning and, since much of this lab. work was research on dysentery, the atmosphere of his bedroom wasn't too pleasant. He also acted as unofficial night-nurse; all the seriously ill children lay in rooms leading off his own, and he was frequently called to attend to complicated cases. But despite the numerous difficulties encountered when practising medicine in Dharamsala Oliver was already, within a fortnight, as enthusiastic about the Tibetans as I was soon to become.

During lunch Juliet instructed me in the geography of the camp. It was divided into three sections—Upper Nursery,

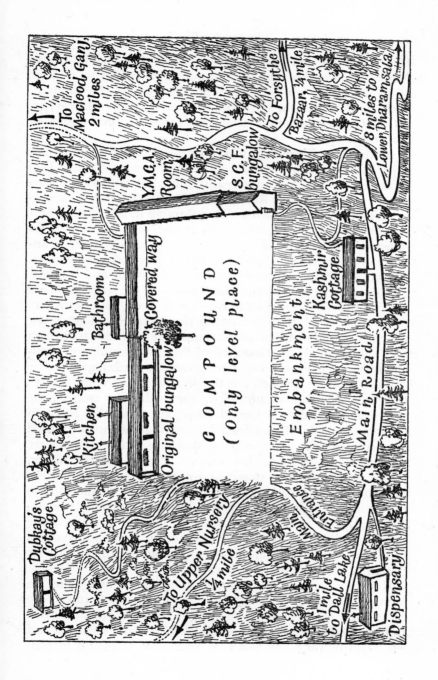

Lower Nursery and Kashmir Cottage (see sketch). The Upper Nursery consisted of a group of ramshackle buildings a quarter of a mile higher up the mountain where about 380 children, aged eight to sixteen, were looked after by Doris Murray, an S.C.I. Quaker volunteer who had come to Dharamsala in November 1962.

At the Lower Nursery, where we lived, some 600 children from one to eight years old were packed into five rooms. Two of these rooms had been recently built, but already the dormitory roof leaked so badly that during the monsoon umbrellas were needed when walking through it. The second new building had been designed as a recreation hall, with a stage for dancing, but because of overcrowding it was now used as another dormitory. It had no beds, which horrified some visitors, though in fact the children were perfectly happy and comfortable sleeping in rows on the wooden floor of the stage. Beds are not essential for Tibetans and can actually be a nuisance where bed-bugs abound; the wood-panelled walls of the old bungalow which formed the nucleus of the camp were swarming with them and unfortunately they soon solved their overpopulation problem by emigrating to the new rooms and to our bungalow.

The Dispensary, which was the pivot of all our work, was an extremely dilapidated bungalow, approached by crossing the road and descending the usual steep path to another ledge on the mountainside. It contained five small rooms; two were used as wards, where as many as eighty dangerously ill children were sometimes crowded together, one was the Dispensary proper, where medicines were stored and outpatients received attention, and the two narrow rooms at the back were allocated to Oliver and the Dispensary ayahs. These three young women, Nema, Lhamo and another Kesang, had all received some nursing training at Safdarjang Hospital in Delhi and spoke a little English, though not enough to avoid frequent linguistic crises in the course of a day's work.

Kashmir Cottage was another dilapidated bungalow, an hour's walk from the Lower Nursery. There about 120 six- to eight-year-olds were in the charge of a Tibetan woman named Dolma, who spoke fluent English. Both she and Chumba had left Tibet in 1954 and had been profitably employed in Calcutta before forfeiting their jobs to help at Dharamsala. When necessary Dolma brought the children who were in her care up to the Dispensary and every week Oliver and Juliet went down to inspect them.

We had just finished lunch when Doris Murray paid us a brief visit. I now think of this extraordinary woman as being in a category apart from the average refugee-worker, for she possesses a combination of qualities which in another age might well have caused her to be revered as a saint. She was not among the Tibetans to escape from an uncongenial background, to enjoy a well-paid job in exotic surroundings, or because this was an interesting new experience. She worked here to serve humanity and though this motive may sound uncomfortably sentimental its results, when seen in action, make the ordinary helper feel very humble indeed. Doris has written to me:

'I believe in a world community. I believe in the mystery of life of which each religion reveals one facet. I believe that words are symbols, counters of common coinage used to express the meaning which lies behind, and to worship the symbol is idolatry. I believe in working where there is need—differences of race, colour, religion are incidental.'

With dignity and discretion she kept aloof from the endless petty squabbling which bedevils life in Tibland, and though the more unsavoury members of the Tibetan ruling clique repeatedly took advantage of her forbearance she was adept at devising excuses for their unpleasantness. Doris had come to Dharamsala to teach, but when she found the health problem so appalling she temporarily discarded her original intention and undertook what most fully trained nurses would consider an impossible task. But all the time she was quietly deepening her knowledge of Tibetan culture, since she hoped eventually to be free to work out that synthesis between Eastern and Western educational systems which she recognized as essential for the children's future. Her bed-sittingroom-cum-dispensary at the Upper Nursery was cramped, dark and rat-infested and she lived on the usual S.C.I. allowance of one and sixpence a day. Doris spoke less than any of us about the lovableness of Tibetans, yet she did more to help them than all the rest of us put together.

# 1

## *Refuge in Dharamsala*

### 30 JULY 1963

I got off to a gruesome start this morning. When we arrived at
the Dispensary at 5.30 a.m. my first job was to put two children,
who had died during the night, into the cardboard boxes which
serve here as coffins. They were both four-year-olds but malnutrition had left them as small as an average two-year-old; it's
quite impossible to cure such miserable scraps once they get
measles, bronchitis or dysentery. To make matters worse there
is no possibility of notifying their parents, though the majority
of the children have at least one parent living; so one often finds
a mother or father wandering around the compound searching
for their child, who has died perhaps several months ago,
clutching the pathetic little bag of cheap sweets that was to
have been the reunion present. Most of the parents are working
on the roads in the Chumba or Kulu valleys, and they save up
until they can pay the bus fare to Dharamsala and provide a
few 'extras' for their children.

The Tibetan's religion says that the dead must be given to
one of the four elements—earth, fire, water or air. In Tibet the
custom was to dismember corpses on a 'cemetery' hill-top,
where birds ate them in a few hours, bones and all. This was
considered giving the dead to the air and the custom obviously arose because in Tibet the earth is frozen hard for most of
the year, wood is too scarce a fuel to be used on funeral-pyres
and indiscriminately throwing bodies into rivers is unwise. But
now, in India, Tibetans are cremated like Hindus.


This is our daily time-table, as devised by Juliet. Of course
various adaptations have to be made to meet emergencies.

*5.15 a.m.* Rise, wash and dress. Walk to the Dispensary.

*5.30 a.m.* Take temperatures, distribute cough-mixtures, vitamin pills and calcium and iron tablets. Treat very bad cases of trachoma and conjunctivitis.

*7.30 a.m.* Breakfast while listening to All-India Radio News in English on Juliet's transistor.

*8 a.m.* Bath the worst scabies cases in permanganate of potash and rub them all over with sulphur ointment. Clean out infected ears and treat them with Terramycin drops. Give percussion treatment to pneumonia and severe bronchitis cases. Massage rickets cases with shark liver oil.

*12.30 p.m.* Lunch, for which Oliver joins us at the bungalow.

*1.45 p.m.* Paint lesser scabies with mercurochrome and check all children to see if any urgently need Oliver's attention. (Just needing it is not enough; in these circumstances a child has to be very ill to qualify for the Dispensary.)

*4.15 p.m.* Tea and biscuits in the bungalow.

*4.30 p.m.* As during the two hours before breakfast.

*6.30 p.m.* Cold bath in tin tub, with lots of Dettol in the water to kill any scabies mites acquired during the day.

*7 p.m.* Supper, for which Oliver joins us.

*8 p.m.* Writing letters, diary and articles.

*11.30 p.m.* Bed on the floor in the corner.

I must confess that to-night, after my first day in the camp, I'm feeling as depressed as anyone could be among these jolly Tibetans. It seems to me mathematically impossible that four Europeans, assisted by a handful of overworked, untrained ayahs, could ever make any significant impression on such a mass of misery.

This evening's sunset was most spectacular. After a very wet thunder-stormy day the rain ceased for about an hour and the valley below us was hidden by an expanse of silver cloud. Suddenly the sky became a frenzied conflagration of orange, violet, red and lemon, and in the near distance a solid-looking black cloud wrapped itself round the dark rock of the jutting mountain-side until you couldn't see which was which. In fact so curious were the cloud formations that the whole western sky looked as if it were full of buildings, floating in space.

The weather here suits me—it's just like a warm, wet Irish July—but the humidity complicates our work beyond endurance. There is no way of drying clothes, so the children's garments are either filthy, which leads to more scabies, etc., or damp, which leads to more bronchitis, etc. And of course a humid climate is in itself unhealthy for Tibetans, even if they are living under the best conditions.

This afternoon Mrs Tsiring Dolma, His Holiness's elder sister and the Principal of the Nursery, came down from her office at the Upper Nursery to 'vet' me. She speaks no English but was accompanied by her two henchwomen, Dela and Diki, who were educated in a Darjeeling Convent School and speak perfect English. Mrs Tsiring Dolma welcomed me most cordially and was very sweet and charming and apparently deeply concerned about my comfort while in the camp; she was effusive in her expressions of sympathy for the children and of gratitude to all Western helpers. Obviously she is enjoyably aware of being the Dalai Lama's sister, yet she seems unsure of herself in dealing with foreigners. I noticed that she wears dark spectacles, which effectively disguise all her reactions. Perhaps she finds this convenient at times.

## 3 August

This morning five-year-old Dolma, a most attractive child, died in Juliet's arms while being taken to hospital in His Holiness' jeep. She had been fed through a nasal tube for the past week and we had all longed to save her, as she didn't suffer from that hopeless degree of malnutrition which means that there is no chance of normal health in maturity. But when we saw Juliet returning down the path to the Dispensary, soon after she had left carrying the little blanketed figure, we knew that Dolma was gone.

Poor Oliver was nearly in tears and quite convinced that somehow it was all his fault; he has not yet come to accept the death of a patient as one of the occupational hazards of his profession. Dolma was the fourth child to die within five days so at tea-time a post-mortem was decided on lest some undiagnosed infection should have invaded the camp. Oliver assured me that he and Juliet could easily cope without me, but I'm afraid that his consideration was wasted as I've always wanted to witness a P.M. and had no intention of missing this opportunity.

After supper we set to, having forbidden any Tibetan to enter the Dispensary, hung a blanket over the window, spread count-less newspapers on the table and drenched the room in un-diluted Dettol. The whole thing was extremely dangerous for Oliver; without adequate gloves or instruments the slightest nick in his hand could have proved fatal. In spite of my fondness for the child I was fascinated by the operation; somehow one doesn't connect the corpse that's being cut up with the human being one liked. After three hours' hard work every organ had been removed and dissected, but the examination merely con-firmed that Dolma had pneumonia in both lungs, an enlarged liver and intestines crammed with huge worms—which were still alive. It's astonishing how much a body can contain: when everything was out in a big basin one could hardly believe that it had all fitted into the little space available. Oliver was very scrupulous about replacing every organ in its exact position, after I had baled bowlfuls of blood out of the torso, and then he sewed up the body as neatly as though after an operation. When we had replaced it in its little cardboard coffin he completed the ceremony by reading a short prayer for the dead from his German prayer-book.

## 4 August

It's Sunday to-day so we have a free afternoon and I can write a longer entry. Really these Tiblets are most remarkable—I doubt if 600 children of any other breed could be so easily managed. Indeed it would be impossible to treat their com-plaints even as effectively as we do were it not for their extra-ordinary obedience and conspicuously high average rate of in-telligence—even the tiniest tots respond to sign-language. On my first morning at the Dispensary Juliet decided that we should administer cough-mixture regularly, so I went out to confront the multitude, bearing a huge flagon of mixture and a spoon. Not very hopefully I coughed exaggeratedly myself, pretended to drink from the spoon and indicated the spot on the veranda where I wanted all 'coughers' to queue. My astonishment was considerable when, within two minutes, all concerned were lined up for their dose, beaming at me with that irresistible blend of spontaneous affection and trust so characteristic of small Tibetan children.

Of course the language problem *is* a nuisance at times as none of the children even speak Hindi, which Juliet would be able to understand. Neither she nor I hope to learn more than a few basic medical phrases in Tibetan, but Oliver, with his Swiss gift of tongues, is making rapid progress and should soon have a good working knowledge of his patients' language. I envy him this facility, as it will enable him to get closer to the Tibetans than most Europeans do; already his sensitivity to their point of view has won him the affection and confidence of both adults and children.

There are two hamlets of tumble-down shacks near here— Forsythe Bazaar and Macleod Ganj—which have been taken over fairly recently by the refugees. Hitherto these adults have been wary of Western medicine, preferring their own 'amchis', who use a combination of herbal lore and quasi-religious charms—but now the sick from both hamlets are coming to the Dispensary in increasing numbers during 'out-patient' hours. Perhaps this is partly because Oliver sincerely respects their religious beliefs and also studies the old herbalist medicine; he believes in using simple local remedies when possible, rather than in concentrating on exorbitantly expensive drugs from abroad.

To return to the Distinguishing Marks of Tiblets. Their consideration for and politeness to each other positively makes me feel I've moved to another planet. I haven't yet seen them quarrelling over anything—a most striking example of how deeply the Buddhist doctrine of non-violence has influenced the race. Not that Tibetans are incapable of quarrelling; many of them, especially the Khambas, have very hot tempers, and when drunk on chang or arak (their beer and spirits) they quite happily resort to fisticuffs. But fundamentally they are neither aggressive nor vindictive and their quarrels are always short-lived. In Simla I watched a practice soccer match between some

of the boys at Chota Simla School and there wasn't one deliberate foul in the whole sixty minutes. Moreover, if a boy accident-
ally fouled he stopped playing immediately and apologized to
his opponent. Incidentally, Tibetans seem to be wonderful
natural footballers, though the idea of organized team sports is
foreign to them, and this school recently beat five others to win
the regional championship.

But the most endearing of all the Tiblets' unusual traits is
their generosity, which seems particularly impressive when one
remembers how very little they have to be generous with. If a
parent brings buns or sweets the lucky child will often divide
them up and hand them round to those near by—without any
prompting from anybody. Similarly, when I go on my rounds
in the Dispensary with special foods for certain cases, the privileged patient will take a few mouthfuls and then point to those
whom he considers are being unfairly neglected. It's indescribably touching to see a worried five-year-old sitting up in bed
looking from his mug of savoury soup to the mugs of soggy rice
given to the others and emphatically indicating his disapproval
of this injustice, before finishing his meal with an obviously
guilty conscience. Unfortunately I can't explain that food suitable for one case would kill another, so even those who can feed
themselves have to be supervised at meal-times or the sharing of
sieved spinach with dysentery cases might have fatal results.
Some Tibetan children have already been sent to Europe and
others are to follow soon. I dread to think of the effect our
civilization will have on them.

Most Tiblets don't seem to form any special friendships: they
play or chat together indiscriminately. Europeans often remark
on their lack of playfulness, in our sense of the word, and attri-
bute it to malnutrition. Obviously there is an element of physical lethargy involved, but I feel that some visitors to refugee
camps over-stress this and misinterpret it as a symptom of
misery, forgetting that Tiblets are not as restless as Western
children and can be perfectly happy sitting immobile for hours
on end, talking to each other quietly but animatedly. Yesterday
provided a good example of the inherent self-discipline of these
youngsters. Before lunch I captured Sonam Dorje, aged about
six, and laid him on a bed in position for percussion treatment.

Then Oliver called me to help fix a drip on an emergency case
so I abandoned Sonam Dorje, taking it for granted that he'd
amuse himself until my return—but when I came back three-
quarters of an hour later he was still lying exactly as I'd placed
him, wide awake yet quite content to await developments for as
long as might be necessary. And he is certainly suffering from
no lack of energy, because when I'd finished tapping him he
romped off and was soon to be seen aiming stones at a target
rock down the mountain-side.

All the children have names, except one chubby two-year-old
who was found a year ago beside the body of his dead mother in
Kalimpong. (I have now christened him 'Ming Mindu'—'The
Nameless One'!) However, there are no family names in Tibet,
apart from the nobility, and the range of Tibetan names—
which are often common to both sexes—is strictly limited, so
each child has a number written on a piece of cloth which is
hung round its neck. Many Tiblets also wear as 'necklaces' a
picture of His Holiness and a piece of red cloth blessed by a
High Lama and guaranteed to protect them from evil.

The chief complaints here are bronchitis, pneumonia, T.B.,
whooping-cough, chicken-pox, measles, mumps, amœbic and
bacillary dysentery, round-, hook-, tape- and wireworms,
scabies, septic headsores from lice, septic bed-bug bites, boils,
abscesses of incredible sizes, rickets, bleeding gums, weak hearts,
asthma, conjunctivitis, trachoma and otitis media. The majority
suffer from calcium and vitamin C deficiency and a heartbreaking number, no matter what is done for them now, will
probably be partially blind or deaf, or both, in maturity. I was
quite relieved by the deaths of three out of the four who went
this week: it was obvious that they would have died young anyway, after a few more years of suffering. Worms are the main
immediate cause of death. Juliet tells me that soon after she
arrived she witnessed the unforgettably horrible sight of a four-
teen-inch-long worm coming out of a year-old baby's mouth.
Naturally enough the child was choked to death. In extreme
cases the worms sometimes infest even the brain. Scabies, which
we tend to think of as a mildly annoying skin disease, is almost
equally serious under these conditions of malnutrition, overcrowding and dirt. Many of the children are so covered with

festering, open sores that you couldn't find room for a sixpence on a clear bit of skin. And when put to bed—six children lie across each bed—the heat so aggravates the itch and pain that they often lie awake whimpering quietly for hours. The only effective answer to scabies is cleanliness, but until the monsoon is over we are helpless to do anything about this. We can only try to keep the suppurating sores under some sort of control, and here again, if the Tiblets weren't so co-operative our task would be almost impossible.

Each afternoon when Juliet, Kesang and I go out onto our bungalow veranda we find five queues—one from each room—awaiting us in charge of their respective ayahs. We are then joined by two of the Dispensary ayahs, and for the next three hours there isn't time to raise one's eyes from the succession of naked little bodies. The children take off their filthy dress or shirt and trousers, just before their turn comes, and many of them have to be painted all over with mercurochrome. Others are infected only in certain places and it's pathetic to see tiny tots of three or four helpfully and solemnly indicating their sore patches, from the tops of their shaven heads to between their toes. It's even more pathetic to see some of them comparing scabies, as our children might compare stamp collections, while they wait in the queue. But then, they don't know what good health feels like, so perhaps their suffering is not as ghastly as we imagine. Sometimes, during my first couple of days, I didn't notice *all* the infected areas and if the child concerned failed to put me right the next one would very quickly point out that a place behind this ear or under that arm was being forgotten. Often one comes on a boil or an abscess that needs squeezing out and then a little crowd collects around the sufferer, stroking his back or patting his head to help him through the ordeal. I wish I could show more sympathy to each child during this whole performance, but when dealing with such numbers it's difficult to treat them as individuals. Yet already I'm afraid I have a favourite—which is deplorably unethical of me!

Lunch-time to-day provided a little light relief. Spinach was one of the vegetables, and the last meal Dolma had before her death consisted entirely of spinach—a fact which became very obvious during last night's post-mortem. Accordingly, when the lid came off the vegetable-dish both Oliver and Juliet paled perceptibly, and I—the non-medical member of the party— had three helpings.

Which brings me to the subject of food. Our diet here is about 80% Tibetan—very nice too. All meals come from the camp kitchen, and though the ingredients are local the methods of cooking are not. For breakfast we have an almost European meal of cornflakes bought by Juliet in Lower Dharamsala, pro- cessed cheddar cheese donated to the camp by the Ameri- can Government, hard-boiled eggs and moo-moo—which is steamed, grey-brown Tibetan bread, served in the shape of little dumplings. The lunch and dinner menus are very varied —potatoes (a favourite vegetable in Tibet) cooked in many strange and palatable ways, ordinary vegetables like carrots, cabbage, peas and egg-plant, noodles with unidentifiable little things chopped through them, vegetable salads mysteriously concocted, marvellous goat's meat fritters, curious objects like sour-milk pancakes which I absolutely adore, rice pilaus and savoury dumplings made like swiss rolls filled with meat and onions and unknown herbs. Soup is served, in Tibetan fashion, at the end of the meal and no puddings are provided. But Chumba bakes several different types of delicious bread, on which we spread tinned jam or the excellent local honey. The Tibetans don't normally use curries, I'm thankful to say, and on the whole their food is much more European than anything I've tasted since leaving Bulgaria.

Of course in Tibet itself the average peasant did not have such luxurious meals. His staple foods were meat, milk, tsampa (barley flour) and the very nourishing salted butter-tea—a monotonous but healthy diet. Many people express disapprov- ing astonishment when they hear of Buddhists eating meat, but vegetarianism was never a practical possibility in Tibet, where few crops can be grown; so the herds of yak and sheep have always been the chief source of Tibetan food—which may partly explain why they were such a renownedly healthy race. Some of the lamas and monks did abstain from meat, but most people were content to salve their consciences by somewhat illogically considering butchers as social outcasts and never *ordering* an animal to be killed. If you went to your local butcher's tent and

saw a dead sheep and bought it for your supper you remained
innocent, but if you went along and told the butcher you wanted
a sheep killed for to-morrow's supper you were guilty of causing
life to be taken. The blatant irrationality of this is childish—yet
you could match it in some Christian teachings without having
to think too hard.

The diet of the children here is very different from ours—too
different, I felt at first. Then, on reflection, I realized that al-
though we might feel more at ease if living nearer their level, it
wouldn't help to have us falling sick. Yet I'm not satisfied that
their menu need be quite so bad, considering the various money-
allowances and per capita donations of foodstuffs that are supposed to come to the camp from the Indian Government and
other sources. This is a situation that might profitably be in-
vestigated.

At the moment they get for breakfast half a moo-moo (about
three ounces), which contains very little of food value, and a
small mug of slightly sweetened tea. That is at seven o'clock and
the next meal is at noon, when they get a mug of rice and dahl,
or a half-mug of watery soup containing about an ounce of
meat, with half a moo-moo. Tea at three o'clock is the same as
breakfast, and supper at six o'clock the same as lunch. However,
Juliet has just obtained a special allowance from S.C.F. to provide the Dispensary cases with one piece of fruit each per day,
and she herself will be in sole charge of this fund, so that is one
concrete improvement.


7 AUGUST

To-day Herr Albert Eggler, Honorary Secretary to the Swiss
Association for Tibetan Homesteads, came to Dharamsala, and
Oliver, Juliet and I were invited to the ritual luncheon party
which Mrs Tsiring Dolma holds at the Upper Nursery whenever V.I.P.s visit the camp. Herr Eggler is in India to choose a
third batch of thirty-three Tibetans (mostly adults) for permanent resettlement in Switzerland; the first two batches were
chosen mainly from refugees in Nepal.

This being Wednesday Juliet has her 'day off', which she
spends working at the Kangra Schools, so she declined the

invitation and Oliver and I set off together up the path through the forest. The monsoon was monsooning even more than usual and we were soaked to the skin after the fifteen-minute climb. But the lunch was worth it—a banquet of over a dozen savoury dishes, followed by bowls of delicious soup. The idea is that you drink the soup out of the bowl and then daintily extricate the residue of choice morsels with your chopsticks: but already I'd been so demoralized by the intractability of said chopsticks that I threw etiquette overboard and furtively fished the bits out with my fingers. It's fascinating to watch Tibetans handling these elegant ivory sticks—they can unerringly pick up *one* grain of rice with them. In Tibet they are used only by the nobility, so a surreptitious survey of my fellow-guests soon revealed which individuals had risen from the ranks: if you haven't learned the art from babyhood you can't ever really master it.

Herr Eggler—a famous mountaineer and lawyer—has a delightful sense of humour, and during lunch we amused ourselves by considering the effect polyandry would have on European officialdom. It's a lovely thought; imagine the passport—Name of Husband (add an 's' with pen): Sonam Dorje, Tsiring Sonam, Dorje Chumbe. Name of Wife: Dolma Tsiring. Children's names: (here follows a long list) and then the bemused passport officer asking, 'Whose father is which?' or 'Whose child is which?' depending on the way it struck him. And Dolma Tsiring replying gaily in Tibetan, 'Who knows—and who cares?' Actually, of course, all such children are traditionally accepted in Tibet as being the *eldest* brother's (among the Tibetans the husbands in polyandric marriages are always brothers) and Herr Eggler said the small minority of family units already built on this basis would be allowed to remain intact, though the young people who are settling in Switzerland would have to obey Swiss law and restrict themselves to one partner at a time. To me this seems unfair. It may suit a Tibetan peasant to have two or three husbands simultaneously, whereas a rich European woman may prefer to have two or three in rapid succession, but why should Tibetans be forced to conform to European standards? However, I'm sure this is now a purely academic question, as the social conditions which caused polyandry in Tibet will not obtain in Europe.

A group of ayahs having tea
Kesang, Juliet, the author and Sister Sawnay

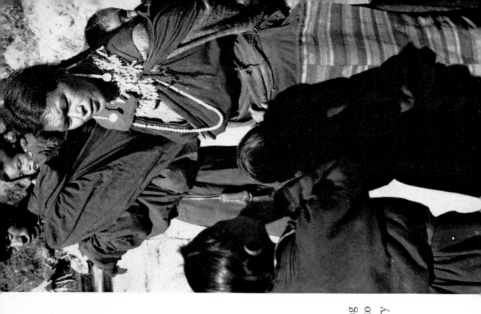

Oliver and Samja,
one of our psychiatric
cases!

Parents bringing
their children to
the nursery

In this camp and the surrounding area Tibetans live together in a virtually uncontaminated Tibetan atmosphere. Apart from the 1,500 who are temporarily settled in Macleod Ganj and Forsythe Bazaar there are also many adults attached to the camp as lamas, cobblers, tailors, weavers, carpenters, cooks and ayahs, so one is able to study them as an ethnic group, though their community life is of course artificial in some ways.

The first thing to impress me when I arrived here was the complete equality between the sexes, a phenomenon which seems all the more remarkable when one has just spent six months in Muslim and Hindu societies. Watching the Tibetans together I could easily believe that I was in a modern Western community and it is salutary to remember that this equality, so new to our society, has always been taken for granted in Tibet. Even in the religious field women can gain the pre-eminence of being regarded as a Bodhisattva, like Pol-den Lha-mo, Abbess of a monastery on the shores of Lake Yamdrok, who is considered to be a special protector of the Panchen Lama and the Dalai Lama. Incidentally, her Sanskrit name, when translated into English, is somewhat startling—'The Adamantine Whore'.

One of the chief joys of my life here is the chanting of the ayahs' night-prayers. These girls assemble near our door to pray from 8.0 to 8.30 p.m. and anything more beautiful you couldn't wish to hear. Normally, Eastern music doesn't move Europeans—at best one is neutral to it, at worst irritated by it—but this chanting really means something to me. It sounds oddly un-Eastern; my personal impression is of a cross between Gregorian Chant and Slav folk-music. And somehow the fact that during the day one has seen these illiterate, filthy young women carrying hundredweight sacks of stores up the steep slopes, laughing and joking among themselves, wiping babies' bottoms, horseplaying with the young men from the Upper Nursery and sitting picking over each others heads for lice, gives a special poignancy to the solemn rhythm and fervent quality of their chanting. People may argue that Lamaism is a corrupt hotch-potch of esoteric teaching, worthless to the average Tibetan peasant, but these ayahs at their prayers belie this. They may *know* very little about their religion, yet unless they *felt* it as a significant force in their lives they could never render

D

these hymns as they do. Even from a purely aesthetic point of view the performance is astonishing: I couldn't help comparing it with the alarming noises that pass for hymn-singing in the average Irish country church. The children also chant their prayers before going to bed and show an equally remarkable talent.

At the Upper Nursery to-day we saw some of the pictures painted by Doris's art-students in the four- to eight-year-old age group. All the exhibits were good and two were quite exceptional. It is noticable that Tiblets have a much bolder approach to design than most Western children, and one immediately suspects that this is the result of their total dependence, for amusement, on their own ingenuity. Watching them playing with scraps of torn paper, bottle-tops, cardboard boxes, bits of tinfoil or sticks and stones, one realizes how damaging our elaborate toys can be. Here the children's minds are kept alert and supple by the continual exercise of inventiveness and they probably get more pleasure from a brightly coloured Vim tin than European children get from a five pound doll or a twenty-five pound toy motor; between dawn and dusk that Vim tin will be a doll, a ball, a steam-roller, a rattle, a boat and a rifle. Oliver tells me that an American tourist visited the camp a week before my arrival and was so appalled by the lack of toys that she promised to send ten crates of the things from New York on her return home. U.S. A.I.D. (Ability for Impeding Development).

## 9 AUGUST

Every day more adults are coming to the Dispensary during out-patient hours and I notice that they have wonderful physiques; both men and women are muscular and well-proportioned and were obviously adequately nourished from birth— unlike the unfortunate present generation of Tibetan children. Most travellers in Tibet before the Invasion remarked on the fact that one rarely saw an underfed Tibetan; in those days the national economy was virtually self-sufficient, with enough surplus grain stored in the Government and Monastery granaries to insure against the occasional emergency caused by bad weather. Throughout recorded history Tibet has never suffered from famine—until the influx of Chinese soldiers and settlers sent prices soaring and wrecked her simple national economy. Judging by results a feudal system, however theoretically deplorable its persistence may have been, was very well suited to the people and conditions of Tibet.

Most of the ills from which Tibetan adults now suffer are brought on by the change of altitude and by their exposure to diseases unknown in the antiseptic climate of Tibet. Naturally they have no resistance to the myriad bugs of India, and their peasant reluctance to adapt habits of clothing and personal hygiene to a hot climate doesn't help. They wear so many clothes and the system of putting them on is so intricate that getting down to skin-level is a day's work. *En route* one encounters a rich variety of lice, fleas and bed-bugs, and as all the refugees' most precious possessions are stored around the waist, in a pouch formed by the upper half of the 'chuba', one has to look out for a shower of little bundles on getting that far. My original sample collection consisted of a few rupees tied up in a rag, a half-eaten lump of moo-moo, a letter addressed by a professional scribe in Tibetan, Hindi and English, a knife, an apple, a wooden cup, a comb, an empty condensed-milk tin and a picture of His Holiness looking somewhat the worse for wear. Having recovered this little lot from the floor I apologized profusely for my clumsiness and the patient nodded and smiled and conveyed the equivalent of 'Not to worry'. I then proceeded with the disrobing, which only took another ten minutes or so— and meanwhile I was counting the fleas and/or lice which were rapidly transferring themselves to a European base. Not surprisingly, the patient is often incapable of re-robing single-handed when the examination is over and another Tibetan must come to the rescue, ending up, if a woman is concerned, by tying the inevitable baby onto 'Amela's' back. With luck it'll be another five years before she has to undress again—and perhaps if we too had grown up in stone huts at 14,000 feet we might have neglected to develop the habit of removing clothes at regular intervals. Yet in Tibet, when doing strenuous outdoor work, both sexes strip to the waist, which doubtless explains why they are so unselfconscious about medical examinations in public. Their dignified acceptance of the process seems

both charming and wholesome; one hopes that Western workers will never try to replace it by our sort of fussy prudery.

To-day we scored a big, but rather sad, victory. Many Tibetan laymen wear their hair in long braids tied over the top of
the head, and for the past week the chief cook from the Palace
has been coming to us daily with an astronomical number of
head-sores caused by infected louse-bites. Oliver gently tried to
persuade him to cut his hair, but he obviously regarded it as
being his crowning glory and there was no surrender—until
this morning, when one of the sores had turned to a vast car-
buncle and that was *that*. I felt so sorry for him, as he sat on a
bench on the Dispensary veranda having those lovely (but oh!
so lousy) locks shorn off, while his wife stood beside him in tears
of sympathy.

# 2

# *Disease and Drama*

A most extraordinary thing happened last night. Yesterday afternoon Jill paid us a surprise visit, on her way back to Delhi, and presented Juliet with a mongrel puppy rescued from the gutters of Dalhousie. As it was a bitch we christened her 'Poomah' (Tibetan for 'girl') and when Jill left she settled down very happily. Then came supper-time: Juliet was in the 'bathroom' and Oliver and I were sitting watching Poomah playing with a stick in the middle of the floor when Chumba, as usual, brought our meal on a big tray. From the doorway he took one look at Poomah and went rigid with fear. Normally he is all beams and greetings but now his face tautened and his eyes went quite glassy with terror. Oliver and I at once realized that this was no ordinary allergy to dogs, since Chumba adores the camp-dog—a big ginger mongrel. And anyway the emotion he showed was not merely physical fear. Meanwhile Poomah had stopped her frisking and was looking doubtfully at Chumba, though Jill had told us that she makes friends rather too indiscriminately. As I stood up to take the tray from Chumba, who obviously wasn't going to come one inch farther, Oliver asked what was wrong, using his best Tibetan. Chumba looked piteously at us, gave a sort of shudder and said: 'Very bad dog!' Then he bolted. Oliver followed and on his return a quarter of an hour later explained that a black dog with a white tip to its tail was the reincarnation of an exceptionally evil man. So poor Poomah had to be banished; apart from anything else we were told that His Holiness would be most upset to hear that such an inauspicious creature was being kept in one of his camps. How true this is I don't know, but I'll never forget Chumba's entry and first sight of Poomah. Something very curious happened to the atmosphere and before Oliver or I had the least idea what it was all about we both sensed the weirdness in the air.

To-day the monsoon has gone mad and turned the whole world to a liquid turmoil—the mountain sliding and slipping in chunks with rumbling roars, cascades of water tearing by on all sides, the road a racing brown torrent, the paths waterfalls and every roof in the place leaking like a sieve. At lunch-time our soup was diluted by raindrops sploshing down from the ceiling of this *new* bungalow and outside it was almost dark, with nothing, nowhere and nobody dry. The monsoon isn't fun at the best of times, but in a refugee camp it's hell. To go out on an evening like this and see rows of children lying on thin sacking laid over damp concrete under a leaking tin roof in a shelter open at both ends, and to listen to the pathetic coughing, would take a tear from a stone. On asking why these children were not in their rooms I was told that they couldn't sleep because of the hoards of vicious bed-bugs which attacked them nightly. Already Juliet has a supply of Tik 20 ready for the anti-bug campaign—but this is a war that can only be waged in dry weather.

13 AUGUST

To-day is Tuesday, my half-day, and I feel that it was uncommonly civil of the monsoon to ease off suddenly at 11 a.m. By the time we had finished lunch the sun was shining and one could see to the horizon—quite an experience after the enclosed greyness of the past fortnight.

This afternoon I walked miles around the mountains on solitary paths that run through a glorious world of giant trees where to-day everything was freshly green and sparkling after the rains. Occasionally I turned some corner which gave me a sudden, grand glimpse of the 16,000 sheer rock range lying immediately north of the camp, with a few obstinate glaciers still unmelted near its summits. These are the peaks visible from the valley floor, but here we are too close to enjoy an unimpeded view.

On my way back to the Nursery I passed Dall Lake, a place of Hindu pilgrimage overlooked by a tiny white temple. In fact the lake is only a lake during this season; throughout the remainder of the year it's a lush green meadow. But to-day the water was over ten feet deep and looked appropriately solemn and sacred, shadowed on three sides by steep, forested slopes.

Here I saw a sunset of matchless beauty. Against the deep blue sky a wide fleet of diaphanous clouds turned to gold, and for minutes there were just those two colours above a hill whose crown of dark green pines stood out sharply against the radiance behind them.

On my way back from the lake to the camp I had a terrifying view of the flooded plains below as the setting sun turned vast areas of water-covered land into glinting sheets of bronze, revealing the uncontrollable ferocity of the swollen rivers: God alone knows what damage is being done down there. Yet here everything quickly returns to normal: already the road that was a torrent yesterday is bone-dry.

After a fortnight here I already feel so much part of the camp that I'm beginning to see how difficult it will be to disengage when the time comes. By now I've got sufficiently into the swing of the work to be able to take a quasi-professional interest in the serious cases, which makes a big difference. Also, having been Jack-of-all-Trades and Master of None during my first week, I decided that under these conditions satisfactory results could be achieved only by concentrating on *one* aspect of the general problem. So, with Juliet's permission, I have taken over the 800 ears of the Lower Nursery—a job any untrained person can do as efficiently as a nurse. My system is to examine carefully every child's ears, note down the name, room number and personal number of the infected cases and treat these daily; the uninfected minority I'll clean out weekly. This is going to be a full-time job, judging by the numbers already on my list.

15 AUGUST

To-day is Indian Independence Day but you would never suspect it here. It's quite a curious sensation to be living *in* but not *with* a country: yet I can't deny that it suits me to live among my Tibetans, high up on a wild mountain with the real India thousands of feet below in the valley.

Yesterday was our third successive fine day so Juliet decided that we should begin the anti-scabies bathing campaign. I wish I could send back a tape-recording of the audible results and a movie-film of the visual ones; we found our choir of angels suddenly transformed into a pack of demons. Tiblets can take unpleasant medicines and lanced abscesses and septic ears and bleeding gums but they will *not* submit to the horrible indignity of personal contact with water.

The camp 'bathroom' consists of a shed some twelve feet by eight, with two cold water taps and a stone floor. There were over 400 children to be washed and six of us to do the job. This would have been difficult enough had the Tiblets been as co-operative as usual, but with each victim screaming its head off and resisting every inch of the way it soon became a nightmare. I don't believe our ear-drums will ever be the same again, and as for our backs—none of us has been able to straighten up since!

Juliet has devised a technique guaranteed to frighten the boldest scabies mite to Kingdom Come. As a start the victim is thoroughly soaped with carbolic and well rinsed under the tap. Next he is steeped for five minutes in a huge tin tub of hot water (from the kitchen) containing generous quantities of permanganate of potash. From this he emerges dyed puce and he is then dried by an ayah before being rubbed all over his sore patches with a foul-smelling, sickly yellow concoction of mustard-oil and sulphur—this final torture being Oliver's contribution to the sadistic orgy. As can be seen, we have an excellently planned strategy—but first you must catch your infant. And I'm sure that never were so many infants so elusive so often as yesterday afternoon. They escaped, panic-stricken, at every stage of the performance—before being undressed, while being soaped (obviously the ideal moment), when placed in the tin tub, while leaving the 'bathroom' to be dried outside and when about to be anointed. In every corner of the camp— and even at points up the hillside—lurked the trembling sacrifices to our zeal; but Juliet and I were inexorable. We had proved that painting with mercurochrome or gentian violet made no impression on the scabies and in future a bath for each child was to be part of the daily régime. So we reckoned that only by rounding up the lot on the first day of the experiment could we hope to break the famous Tibetan stubbornness which we were now seeing in action. The fact that the ayahs were clearly in sympathy with their charges, and regarded us as meddling eccentrics, didn't help—and here too we felt that an initial show of force was very necessary.

Indians usually obey a European's orders if under supervision and they will pretend to agree—even when they don't—with Western ideas; but the independent-minded Tibetans only obey orders from non-Tibetan authorities if they can understand, and approve of, the reasoning behind an order. In this particular case the one way to make them see the logic behind washing the children is to prove that the results are good. So we must resign ourselves to their opposition till time justifies our present 'tough line'. However, though the native independence of Tibetans has disadvantages, it also creates a much more congenial atmosphere than the servility of Indians. One can respect the Tibetans—even at their most exasperating—and personal relationships with them start from a basis of mutually acknowledged equality.

On to-day's evidence we have won the first round of the Bathing Battle. This afternoon the majority of the children accepted their fate—not without protest, but in a manner which tacitly admitted defeat—and the number of attempted escapes was much reduced. The whole operation is certainly a classic example of 'being cruel to be kind' and one can hardly blame the ayahs for resenting the amount of additional pain inflicted on their charges. Yet already the Tibetan genius for making the best of a situation is showing itself. To-day some of the victims, while sitting four at a time in the potassium tub, discovered that it was fun to pour mugs of purple water over each other's heads. But I'm afraid that we workers do not enjoy the performance as we bend for hours over a tub, getting soaked to the skin and slipping on the soapy stone floor, amidst shrieking, writhing, naked little bodies whose number never seems to grow less—until at last the blessed moment comes when the final contingent is in and we realize that there is no longer an immediate replacement for every child we have washed.

18 AUGUST

Sunday again, so I've time to luxuriate in a long entry without losing sleep! I waited till to-day to describe our visit to the theatre on the 14th—an improbable recreation hereabouts, but the group known somewhat formidably as 'The Tibetan Refugees' Cultural Association's Drama Party' has its headquarters near Macleod Ganj and occasionally musical plays are staged to entertain the locally settled Tibetans. During the monsoon such performances are infrequent, as the audience sits on strips of matting in the open air, but on Wednesday we had word sent us that a classical and a modern play would be staged that evening and after supper we set off to walk round the mountain to the theatre.

Dancing and singing were the main recreations in Tibet, as anyone can deduce from the spontaneous skill of the average refugee in these arts. So strong is the national impulse to dance that many centuries ago it became interwoven with the national adaptation of Buddhism and most people have heard of the lengthy ritual dances—often inaccurately called 'Devil Dances' —of the Lamas. The legendary origin of these dances was a 'thunderbolt dance in the skies' of the Guru Padma Sambhava when he had exorcised all evil influences from the site chosen for the first Tibetan monastery at Samye. Since that date it seems that the study of the esoteric Tantric texts has been accompanied by a dramatizing of their teaching through sounds, postures and rhythmic movements of great variety. These ceremonial dances are as numerous as the texts, and each sect of Tibetan Buddhism uses its own forms, emblems, masks and figures. Obviously such dances could never be understood without a considerable knowledge of the exceedingly complex philosophy which they were evolved to express. Many of them were originally severe mental and physical disciplines through which men attempted to reach a state of supreme mystical exaltation and—as in ancient Greece and Egypt—only the initiated could witness or participate in these rituals. But now they are publicly performed on special occasions and in the majority of cases their symbolism is not fully understood even by the Lama dancers themselves.

In a sense, therefore, the peasant folk-dances and songs are at present a more vital and genuine part of Tibetan culture than the stylized, semi-meaningless monastery dances. Up to the time of the Chinese invasion these folk-arts were richly alive and always developing throughout the country. Just as Ireland or England have their village hurling or cricket teams, who play in regional championships, so Tibet had her village dancers and singers, who gathered about once a month in a chosen village to stage a competition. Characteristically, there were no prizes, nor was there any cult of individual 'star' performers—the winner was simply the village whose team received the most enthusiastic applause. During the festival of the Tibetan New Year—which falls on the day of the February full moon and is the great national holiday—the villages of an area sent their best team to the nearest town for the big annual competition.

These singers and dancers were always amateurs and it was considered very bad form to turn professional; but naturally the required talents were often inherited and certain families were renowned for their ability. In such cases the father usually taught not only his own children but those other local youngsters who showed signs of talent.

The Tibetans had songs to accompany each everyday task and in some cases to accompany the separate parts of one task —e.g. masons had special songs for laying foundations, building walls and putting on roofs. In the fourteenth or fifteenth century of our era dances were composed to go with these songs and both the dances and the costumes of the men and women differ conspicuously in the three chief provinces of Döme, Döte and Utsang: there are also many minor regional differences. Most of the songs refer to the vast beauty of the Tibetan landscape but love-songs are only sung at marriage festivals, which indicates what we would call a lack of emotional involvement in sexual relationships; it certainly does not signify any prudish traditional policy of shielding the young from temptation. A similar lack has been noted among the Buddhist Sherpas by Professor Fürer von Haimendorf, who deduced it from the absence of domestic friction which he observed in polyandric households. It certainly helps to explain that happy-go-lucky Tibetan attitude to sex—as a cross between a good meal and

an exhilarating game—which results in a proliferation of
warmly welcomed bastards in many refugee camps. Babies are
things that *will* happen and no one fusses.

The importance to the Tibetans of their dances and songs is
stressed by the fact that very soon after the 1959 exodus to India
the Dalai Lama asked his Cabinet to make an attempt to keep
this part of the Tibetan culture alive. At first glance such a
preoccupation might seem frivolous, considering the conditions under which the average refugee was then living; but,
in fact, His Holiness showed commendable realism in acting so promptly. He knew that refugees need more than food
and clothing and that a living art could soon die if the steady
transmission of skill from generation to generation were not
maintained.

In September 1959 some of the more expert refugee dancers
met in Kalimpong to tackle the enormous problem of starting
a drama group without instruments, costumes, masks—or
money. Indian craftsmen couldn't make instruments which they
had never seen, but eventually, through India's Representative
in Tibet, a few instruments were brought out over the border
and some others were smuggled into Sikkim and Nepal, *en route*
for Kalimpong. Meanwhile the seven founder-members of the
Drama Party were collecting songs from natives of all the
Tibetan provinces and sending around the camps to find children suitable for training. Soon about twenty boys and girls
had joined the group and for the next six months they worked
hard eight hours a day, not able to afford even a cup of tea
during their long practice sessions.

The Drama Party's first public performance was given in
1960 at Kalimpong, and its success provided enough money for
new costumes. Next they were invited to perform before the
Afro-Asian Conference in Delhi, where their skill was much
appreciated, and when His Holiness moved to Dharamsala he
suggested that they also should make this their headquarters.
By now the group's fame had spread throughout the refugee
world and many parents sent specially talented children to
Dharamsala, where they received some conventional schooling
as well as their specialized training.

At the moment, apart from performing the traditional Tibetan dances, the group also stages two dramas; one depicting the coming of Buddhism to Tibet and the other the coming of Communism. The first of these was recently written by a learned Lama who adapted ancient songs and dances to fit his presentation of the historical events of the eighth century. After many rehearsals this play had its first performance before His Holiness, members of the 'Kashag' (the Tibetan Cabinet) and many guests. A little later the Drama Party successfully toured Delhi, Calcutta and Darjeeling, raising quite a lot of money for distribution among the worst-off refugees. It is now their ambition to produce several more plays illustrating incidents from Tibetan history and to tour extensively in India, and possibly abroad.

On Wednesday evening most of the camp ayahs took time off to attend the drama, and as Oliver and I walked to Macleod Ganj (Juliet was still in Kangra doing her half-day duties) groups of singing young women preceded and followed us along the road, their clear voices filling the forest with melody. From Macleod Ganj to the theatre a rough sloping track—blocked at one point by a new landslide—curves around the mountain, overlooking a deep, wooded valley on the right. Now we were walking among a stream of Tibetans, many carrying sleeping babies on their backs or accompanied by toddlers trotting sturdily behind them, all in high spirits at the prospect of the evening's entertainment.

I find it very difficult to define the essence of Tibetan charm. Anyway charm is too soft and smooth a word—let's just say likeability. Generalizations are rash, but not always avoidable, and I don't think anyone who knows the Tibetans will deny that they have a most distinctive and attractive racial personality. It seems to be compounded of resilient happiness, a peculiarly innocent fearlessness that shows in their direct, steady gaze, a quick sense of humour and an infectious zest for simple pleasures that makes one feel more alive in their company.

To all this their picturesque everyday attire adds an essentially irrelevant but delightful 'finishing touch'. The men's high fur caps or broad-brimmed hats show off their strong and often very handsome features and the nigger-brown chuba, usually drawn up around the waist to kilt-length, gives a sort of dignified swagger to their gait as they move easily up the steep

mountain paths to which their gaily coloured, knee-length cloth
boots are ideally suited. Normally a knife, spoon and leather
silver-embossed pouch containing flint and steel in lieu of
matches are attached to their belts, and sometimes a short
sword in a marvellously ornate sheath is also thrust into the
belt. A silver reliquary is usually hung round their necks and
those who enjoy a certain standing in Tibet wear shoulder-
length turquoise ear-rings in the left ear.

The women look no less splendid with their long gowns and
richly striped aprons and waist-long hair, the braids interwoven
with coloured threads. They wear masses of heavy silver and
turquoise and coral jewellery, carrying all the invested wealth
of the family on their persons. But now some are entirely without ornament because misfortune has forced them to avert
starvation by selling their only remaining possessions. Yet however hard their lot they all retain their wooden prayer-beads,
worn around the wrist, and those silver prayer-wheels which
they carry everywhere.

I particularly love seeing the children in exact miniature
replicas of their parents' clothes—they look so much more
pleasing than the Western-style garments donated from abroad
for our Tiblets at the camp.

On arriving at the theatre Oliver and I were given cushions
of honour in the front row; it was impossible to decline them,
yet I would have much preferred to sit among the body of the
audience. Immediately behind us, sharing the shelter of what
might be described as the proscenium of the covered stage, sat
the Palace officials and a number of lamas; but everyone else
was squatting cross-legged under the sky, quietly waiting for the
curtain to rise. On our right, as we faced the stage, was a large
mural illustrating with crude realism the various atrocities inflicted by the Chinese on the Tibetans, and on the left was the
usual shrine consisting of a large photograph of the Dalai Lama
—the frame draped in white scarves—with a row of little
butter-lamps flickering on the shelf beneath it.

When the curtain rose we saw as backdrop a painting of the
Potala, with many details characteristic of Tibetan daily life in
the foreground. The picture was reminiscent of a European
Primitive and showed none of the delicate craftsmanship associ-

ated with Oriental pictorial art: but this is explained by the fact that in Tibet no tradition of painting could develop among the ordinary people, since all such art was religiously inspired and its practice regarded as an esoteric ritual.

As the curtain went up the electricity supply failed, but was rapidly restored, and then we heard the chanted invocation to Chenrezig—Lord of Boundless Love—which precedes every performance. Next three men, representing the chief Tibetan provinces, stood silently in the centre of the stage holding the national flag with its fabulously colourful and intricate design. The spiritual symbolism of this design is too involved for me to understand, much less explain, but it struck me as very appropriate that whereas most countries are satisfied with a pattern of geometrically arranged colours Tibet must have an exuberant wealth of pictorial emblems. As the flag was being presented we heard from behind the scenes that most moving air, 'Kata-tampa'—a very ancient tune adopted as the national anthem in the reign of the 13th Dalai Lama, when its patriotic words were composed. Then, after the standard-bearers had marched off, the play began.

I had been asked by S.C.I. to report on this company's possible appeal to Western audiences and I had no hesitation in encouraging them to take it abroad. The classical drama provides gay, vigorous, graceful dancing, interwoven with quiet scenes revealing the formal beauty of oriental etiquette, and its pleasing music is immediately intelligible to Westerners. The magnificent costumes alone are an aesthetic treat, with their striking originality of design and ornament and their boldly contrasting textures and colours.

We soon realized that we were seeing folk-art of a quality now extinct in Europe. This dancing was not something rescued out of the wreckage of individual national cultures and artificially preserved but was an art-form still fulfilling its original purpose—to give expression to the creativity of unlettered peasants, while instructing a new generation in the history and legends of their race. These performances are a palpable extension of the spiritual and emotional life of the audience and they provide the Westerner with an entirely novel experience. Inevitably such an experience could not be fully shared by members of an all-Western audience, but careful handling of the players throughout the tour should ensure that the essential vitality survives.

The production is not amateurish in the sense of a rural dramatic society playing Goldsmith, yet by our standards it is perceptibly rough around the edges; a Western group with half the talent could give a more technically polished performance. However, attempts to achieve a greater degree of smoothness would destroy that disarming unselfconsciousness which is one of the main attractions of the performance. The players are obviously unaware of being 'specialists', in a category apart from the audience, and the feeling is of a big party at which a few of the guests have suddenly decided to 'do something' to divert their fellows. This was delightfully illustrated when King Tht-Srong-Detsen, during a scene in which he was preoccupied by profound philosophical considerations, casually wiped his nose on the gorgeously embroidered sleeve of his robe. One knows that this is exactly what the original King Tht-Srong-Detsen would have done if the need arose.

I'm less confident about the second drama's popularity abroad. Personally I enjoyed it as much as the first production, but it is difficult to be objective when one has seen it while sitting among people to whom it is the re-enactment of a personal tragedy. It could be regarded as propaganda, if judged exclusively on the political level. Yet seen immediately after the drama on the coming of Buddhism to Tibet it seemed to me that here we were merely witnessing folk-art in the making. One feels that if both these productions are taken abroad the performances should be given on the same evening with only a short interval, so that their basic affinity could be appreciated. Optimists can then reflect that if by some happy chance Tibetan culture is preserved this drama will be part of it three hundred years hence. And pessimists can sadly savour it as the worthy culmination of a great artistic tradition, doomed by the events it depicts.

The acting in this production was superb—so good that during the earlier scenes one simply lived with the family concerned through all their terror and suspense. At first it seemed that these impeccable performances must be due to the exiled actors'

Lower Nursery children, heads shaven as protection from lice infestation
Upper Nursery children, Dharamsala

Sonam Nobo being admired by his elders
Dubkay helping with the anti-scabies laundry
They are getting used to being washed!

sympathetic identification of themselves with the characters—
yet the Chinese soldiers were equally brilliantly portrayed. And
the term 'brilliant' is justified, for this play, which could well
degenerate into melodrama of the 'Titus Andronicus' variety,
provides a severe test of ability. Too crude a gesture, too violent
a reaction or too shrill a voice could ruin everything, but though
the necessary intensity was maintained throughout each harrowing incident emotions were never exaggerated. As the two
daughters of the hero and heroine stood rigidly in a corner,
their faces hidden, while the Chinese soldiers argued about what
should be done with them, all the girls' tension was transmitted
to the audience by a clenching and unclenching of the hands
and a few furtive, affectionately protective gestures towards
each other—a stroke of genius in the same class as King Lear's
oft-repeated 'Never!'

During these scenes I occasionally glanced at the audience
and was moved to see the men and women of the older generation quietly weeping—though even here that curiously mis-
placed laughter, common to theatre audiences all the world
over, was heard amongst the younger generation.

Unfortunately the climax *is* blatant propaganda and dramatically inept; if the play ended with the scene where the guerrillas swear to regain Tibetan independence there would be a
sense of dignity and hope. Yet I feel that we should not apply
our standards to such a drama. The final scene, portraying the
defeat of numerous Chinese soldiers by a handful of Tibetan
guerrillas, gives a disingenuous twist to history—but the audience take immense pleasure from the mowing down of the
Chinese. Everyone claps wildly, shouts encouragement to the
guerrillas and laughs uproariously at the Chinese 'corpses' lying
strewn about the stage—while the boys stand up and pretend
to fire imaginary guns in support. Clearly this catharsis is necessary to the refugees and we are hardly justified in criticizing
anything that relieves or consoles them.

On the way down to Macleod Ganj Oliver and I again enjoyed
many of the songs from the plays, as the audience enthusiastically provided encores. In the Bazaar we caught up with a
party of ayahs and urged them to accompany us via the Top
Road to the Nursery, which is shorter than the Low Road

E

through Forsythe Bazaar. But no—they insisted that the Top Road was haunted by countless evil spirits and were definite that they would prefer to go the long way round. So we set out to brave the demons on our own—though the only ones that worried us were the savage Himalayan bears, which are by far the most dangerous animals in India and are unnervingly numerous around here.

On our way we saw a spectacular display of blue sheet lightning playing along the southern horizon, throwing its wavering, uncanny brilliance into the depths of the Kangra valley.

# 3

# *The Book of the Dead*

It's been very wet again these last few days but we're keeping up the bathing routine. The annoying thing is that the children's clothes can't be washed yet, because of the weather, and as the scabies-mite secretes itself in the seams of garments there's no hope of conquering the disease until it's possible to boil the clothes regularly. On the whole we find it best not to stop and think about the overwhelming numbers we're coping with—it's so disheartening to know that even though we are all working all out all day most of the children are being neglected in some respect. One gets fonder and fonder of them on closer acquaintance.

Yesterday afternoon, when I was writing here in our room, a five-year-old boy-friend came to visit me. (Juliet was out: otherwise he wouldn't have been admitted.) Having exchanged the normal civilities and made the required sympathetic comments on his scabies-infested behind (the poor little devil can hardly sit down) I gave him a banana and resumed writing while he explored the room. Then he approached me again and picking up my box of matches opened it upside down so that all the matches fell out. I feigned not to notice but immediately he picked up every match, looking carefully around to make sure that none were lost and, having replaced them in the box, put it back beside me. In my experience you never have to tell a Tiblet the correct thing to do—they know it already. Which almost makes one believe in reincarnation!

This particular Tiblet—a skinny little chap, loaded with disease—is the one to whom my heart has been lost, against all the rules. Granted it *is* wrong to have favourites: from both the workers' and children's points of view it could easily lead to real unhappiness. Yet when one Tiblet attaches himself to you quietly but firmly such counsels of perfection are soon forgotten. The best I can do now is to refrain from giving Cama Yishy preferential treatment when dispensing food or treats—which will be easy, as I myself don't wish to discriminate, nor does Cama Yishy seek favours of this kind. Already it's recognized in the camp that we are special buddies but no resentment or jealousy is ever shown on that account. It's almost as though the rest of the children know intuitively that I don't love them any the less for being attached to him in a rather different way. He accompanies me on my 'ear-rounds' from room to room, and if for some reason I happen to appear at an unexpected time, when he is not on the scene, the other eight or nine Tiblets, who habitually form my 'Personal Bodyguard', will shout for him and leave a space vacant on the bench beside me, fully accepting his right to sit closest to 'Amela'.

In comparison with other Tiblets Cama Yishy is reserved and undemonstrative though his occasional outbursts of affection have an intensity rare among these children. At times it's very difficult to believe that he's only four or five years old. (One never knows a Tibetan's exact age: this was a matter of little importance in Tibet and ages, if reckoned at all, were counted as from the beginning of the New Year after birth—so a child born at the end of January would be described as a year old when only a fortnight old.) His intelligence is remarkably acute, his thoughtfulness astonishing, his manners have a casual sort of graciousness, his self-possessed gravity—as he sits apparently contemplating The Wheel of Life—is quite startling and, though he's anything but precocious in an unpleasant way, he often gives me the curious feeling of being in the company of an adult.

Almost from the moment of my arrival—long before I had got to know any individual child—Cama Yishy purposefully singled me out and skilfully appropriated a ridiculous amount of my affection before I had realized what was happening. In this sense I did not 'make a favourite' of him—he made himself a favourite of mine. Yet that is really a silly distinction; clearly our mutual affection developed because we each had something the other lacked—as happens in most human relationships that matter. Cama Yishy's need to belong securely to one person was for some reason greater than that of the other Tiblets, who usually appear to be satisfied by affectionate cuddles from all and sundry. This need of his can also be deduced from the fact that, unlike most Tiblets, he has a special friend who came with him to the camp about a year ago—since when neither of them has seen their parents.

Now Cama Yishy delights in helping me by fetching things I need, counting pills—which he does very seriously and efficiently—and generally acting as my lieutenant in organizing the impossibly long queues of ear-cases and in tracking down children who should be in their room-queues but aren't. Frankly, I can't feel too guilty about our friendship. Whatever the heartache on both sides when we part, I know that we will have given each other something valuable, and I can't believe that it would have been kinder to 'slap him down' at the outset— even if I were temperamentally capable of doing so. Life would be just a neutral wasteland if one always ran away from the joys of love merely because one knew that pain and grief might be involved too.

20 August

I must admit that I tend to smile at the notion of not killing a louse because it might be your grandmother. Yet my conversations with English-speaking Tibetans have revealed that their imaginations can deal more effectively with the concept of reincarnation than ours can with the theory of an immortal soul —though they do get rather bogged down when they come to consider Nirvana, since the sort of freedom which it promises is not among the natural desires of human nature. It's interesting to observe how much closer the Buddhist vision of an afterlife is to the Christian view than either is to the Muslim— despite the similarities of Islam and Christianity. And one can't deny that were an objective choice possible the Muslim paradise is the one most people would choose as their final destination.

Many Westerners, including myself, can't resist the temptation to be unkindly witty at the expense of the theory of reincarnation, yet in our more fair-minded moments we must admit that it merits as much serious consideration as any other attempt to explain Man's destiny. And in fact, when it is presented coherently by someone like the Venerable Dr Walpola Rahula, non-committed people who believe in some form of spiritual force may well agree that there 'could be something in it'.

Dr Rahula writes:

. . . a being is nothing but a combination of physical and mental forces or energies. What we call death is the total non-functioning of the physical body. Do all these forces and energies stop altogether with the non-functioning of the body? Buddhism says 'No'. Will, volition, desire, thirst to exist, to continue, to become more and more, is a tremendous force that moves whole lives, whole existences, that even moves the world. This is the greatest force, the greatest energy in the world. According to Buddhism, this force does not stop with the non-functioning of the body, which is death; but it continues manifesting itself in another form, producing re-existence which is called rebirth.

Now another question arises: If there is no permanent, unchanging entity or substance like Self or Soul, what is it that can re-exist or be reborn after death? Before we go on to life after death, let us consider what this life is, and how it continues now. What we call life . . . is the combination of the Five Aggregates, a combination of physical and mental energies. These are constantly changing; they do not remain the same for two consecutive moments. Every moment they are born and they die. 'When the Aggregates arise, decay and die, Obhikkhu, every moment you are born, decay and die. Thus, even now during this lifetime, every moment we are born and die, but we continue. If we can understand that in this life we can continue without a permanent, unchanging substance like Self or Soul, why can't we understand that those forces themselves can continue without a Self or a Soul behind them after the non-functioning of the body?

When this physical body is no more capable of functioning, energies do not die with it, but continue to take some other shape or form, which we call another life. In a child all the physical, mental and intellectual faculties are tender and weak, but they have within them the potentiality of producing a full-grown man. Physical and mental energies which constitute the so-called being have within themselves the power to take a new form, and grow gradually and gather force to the full.

As there is no permanent, unchanging substance, nothing passes from one moment to the next. So quite obviously, nothing permanent or unchanging can pass or transmigrate from one life to the next. It is a series that continues unbroken but changes every moment. The series is, really speaking, nothing but movement. It is like a flame that burns through the night: it is not the same flame nor is it another. A child grows up to be a man of sixty. Certainly the man of sixty is not the same as the child of sixty years ago, nor is he another person. Similarly, a person who dies here and is reborn elsewhere is neither the same person, nor another. It is the continuity of the same series. The difference between death and birth is only a thought-moment: the last thought-moment in this life conditions the first thought-moment in the so-called next life, which, in fact, is the continuity of the same series. During this life itself, too, one thought-moment conditions the next thought-moment. So from the Buddhist point of view, the question of life after death is not a great mystery, and a Buddhist is never worried about this problem.

As long as there is this 'thirst' to be and to become, the cycle of continuity goes on. It can stop only when its driving force, this 'thirst', is cut off through wisdom which sees Reality, Truth, Nirvana.

As the latter part of this exposition implies, Buddhism holds a man entirely responsible for his own spiritual development, in direct opposition to the Christian teaching that he is dependent on Divine Grace for the right use of his Free Will. It is this recognition of what Carl Jung calls the 'self-liberating power of the introverted mind' that impresses a Westerner as the most valuable—to him—ingredient of Buddhism, and though it would be psychologically impossible for most people bred in our traditions genuinely to embrace Buddhism there is no reason why the limitations of Western extroversion should not be corrected by an acquaintance with Eastern introversion.

For those who cannot bring themselves to regard seriously the transmigration of human souls to animal bodies there is an alternative interpretation of the doctrine of rebirth held by leading Buddhist philosophers in opposition to the popular belief. This interpretation, as given by Dr Evans-Wentz, maintains that

> just as the physical seed of a vegetable or animal organism . . . is seen by the eyes to be capable of producing after its own kind only, so with that which figuratively may be called the psychical seed of the life-flux which the eyes cannot see— if of a human being it cannot incarnate in . . . a body foreign to its evolved characteristics.
>
> Degeneration . . . is, of course, concomitant with cultural neglect; but . . . the flowering plant does not degenerate into the apple, nor into the corn, nor one species of animals into another, nor does Man degenerate into anything but the savage man—never into a sub-human creature.

And this view, so obvious to us but so contrary to the majority beliefs of Buddhists everywhere, was strongly upheld by one of Tibet's most distinguished scholars, the late Lama Kazi Dawa-Sandup, who wrote: 'Intellects able to grasp Truth do not fall into the lower conditions of existence.'

However, it is doubtful if this interpretation of the doctrine will ever supersede popular beliefs, with their ban on the taking of life. One result of this ban particularly impresses me here. I've often seen boys catching a moth or beetle or worm, closely but gently examining it and then releasing it completely unharmed; this makes quite a contrast to the attitude of Western boys who, as Shakespeare noted some time ago, delight in torturing such creatures.

21 AUGUST

The most harrowing aspect of life here is the children's emotional suffering. Sometimes one feels that the orphan minority are the best off: they can at least become adjusted to having no family. Parents visit the camp regularly and when they have left one sees anguished little boys and girls looking bewildered and obviously feeling betrayed by their parents' departure without them.

This morning two mothers came, found their little sons (which is not always easy in such a crowd) and then sat under the big tree in the middle of the compound with the boys standing beside them. As I passed on my way to the Dispensary not a word was being spoken or a movement made, but tears were silently streaming down those four faces. Both boys are very bad scabies cases and on seeing me one of the mothers beckoned and pointed to her son's leprous-looking body, gazing up at me with a mixture of reproach and appeal. Then I really wished that I could speak fluent Tibetan, to reassure those women that we were doing all in our power for their children. After tea I saw the mothers going away, looking quite cheerful again. That's the extraordinary thing about Tibetans—despite their soft, affectionate natures they seem able to get on top of a situation that would reduce others to shreds. Yet this doesn't lessen the tragedy of it all; when I say that they looked 'quite cheerful' I mean that they were laughing and talking with the ayahs—but you could still see the unhappiness in their eyes. It isn't difficult to imagine what it must take to stay on top of this sort of situation. And I prefer *not* to imagine the effect of these upheavals on the children.

We had a crisis here to-day. I sensed it at once when I entered the Dispensary this morning and as the hours passed it became increasingly apparent, with teachers, carpenters and cooks frequently going into huddles to discuss something and ayahs sobbing in every second corner. At last Tenzing—one of the teachers from the Upper Nursery, who speaks a little English— came down to explain the mystery to us. Apparently Mrs Tsiring Dolma has just had a row with Mr Kundeling, the Education Minister, and as a result she has flounced off to Delhi, saying she's 'never coming back no more!' All the Nursery staff were called to a special meeting at the Upper Nursery last night to have the news broken to them, and the ayahs, who are deeply devoted to Mrs Tsiring Dolma (whether on religious or personal grounds is a moot point), immediately declared that if *she* wasn't staying here *they* weren't—after which the meeting broke up in disorder. Tenzing thinks that if she doesn't return this camp may be closed within six months. But my personal opinion is that she's bluffing and will return in due course, having made this strategic move to show how essential she is here.

## 22 August

No crises to-day—unless you like to so describe the cutting of the left-hand little finger-nails of all the adults in the camp. Tibetans keep the rest of their nails very short but this is worn about one inch long and used to dislodge nests of nits from each other's heads, to unwax the ears and to excavate the nostrils. Normally Oliver is all for preserving ancient Tibetan customs, but yesterday evening, when he went to the kitchen to photograph the colossal mud stove on which all the camp's food is cooked, he saw Chumba hanging over our dinner, excavating like mad. So this morning I was sent forth at dawn, armed with nail-clippers and instructions to go down fighting—which I very nearly did, as opposition was fierce. I found this a most distasteful chore, since the Tibetans are all absolutely devoted to that long, left, finger-nail—and now how can they cope with the nit-nests, etc.? I felt very tyrannical and without any real justification—after all, if one didn't *brood* on it a few consequences of excavation in the soup (thick veg.) would go unnoticed and do no harm.

I only wish other problems, more serious than long nails, could be as easily solved. About sixty per cent of the children have bleeding gums at the moment as scurvy is one of the commonest results of diet deficiency. Fresh fruit can be had cheaply in this locality and one would imagine that it could be provided regularly; but instead we are dosing the sufferers with vitamin C tablets, which Oliver admits are virtually useless once scurvy has broken out, though they are a help if taken to supplement deficient diet *before* the system has been undermined.

## 27 August

To-day is a very important Hindu festival in this area; thousands come to bathe in the sacred waters of Dall Lake and to worship the serpent-god who dwells near by. During the past week the monsoon has been easing off: now we only have heavy showers each day, with 'long bright periods' in between, and it was clear and sunny at 6.30 this morning when I joined the throngs of pilgrims who were climbing past the camp to the lake.

Somehow I felt more 'with' the Hindus to-day than ever before. These people seemed quite different from the types met with in Delhi; they were very friendly as we ascended the path together and were most anxious that I should go into the temple, ring the snake-god's bell and have the Saddhu put rice on my forehead. (This he did and it stayed on all day, recalling Ash Wednesday!) Such a degree of mateyness seemed very odd; in view of all one reads and hears about the caste system I, as an untouchable, should have been forbidden entry to the temple. But doubtless Gandhi's influence is slowly having its effect, and anyway the enforcement of these rules probably varies widely from district to district. Discrimination against the untouchables—officially re-named the 'Scheduled Castes'— has been made illegal by Article 15 of the Indian Constitution, yet in a country like India it is the influence of the popular reformer that works these changes, rather than the making of new laws.

On my way back to breakfast I reflected that one of India's chief troubles must be the number of half-educated, dis- orientated citizens drifting around her towns and cities. These pilgrims this morning were quite different—honest-to-god(s) peasants with no would-be-Western nonsense about them. One immediate¹⟩ appreciated the sincerity of their faith, however bizarre and unpalatable its outward manifestations. The snag seems to be that Hinduism, though it boasts of its powers of assimilation, cannot in fact successfully survive contact with the modern Western world as, for instance, Islam does. A Muslim may go superficially Western in his speech, dress and material possessions while remaining in his thoughts, feelings and prin- ciples a completely integrated Son of the Prophet. But appar- ently few Hindus can achieve this balance: a veneer of Western education quickly makes them ashamed of their religion and dissatisfied with their country.

30 AUGUST

Another crisis to-day. At 8 a.m. all the staff disappeared without
warning to attend a meeting at the Upper Nursery and they
didn't return until 4 p.m. One result was that the daily bathing
could not take place and I spent the afternoon teaching thirty
of the older boys Gaelic football—an occupation which suited
all thirty-one of us much better than bathing!

The Lower Nursery has two teachers—whose qualifications
to teach anything more than Buddhist hymns are very doubtful
—but this morning they too had vanished and, to my astonishment, I observed two ten-year-old boys doing their job by the
blackboards while the rest of the children squatted cross-legged
on the ground in the usual orderly rows, copying the letters of
the Tibetan alphabet onto their slates with stumps of chalk.
Tiblets possess an innate power of self-discipline, as distinct
from our children's submission to the imposition of discipline
by authority.

At tea-time we heard that, following the mass-meeting, Mrs
Tsiring Dolma has decided to remain here as the Nursery
Principal. Later she visited the Dispensary and was in tears,
which slightly foxed us all. I suppose one really should sympathize with her, despite her genius for alienating even those
who are best disposed towards Tibetan officialdom. Probably
the whole set-up is just too much for a completely uneducated
peasant woman who happens to be His Holiness's sister.

Plans are now going ahead for the building of a new Dispensary. This is essential in the circumstances, yet it's difficult
to get enthused about anything which tends to make these
camps more permanent. 'Tibetan Nurseries' are most emphatically *not* the answer and one longs to see the Tiblets' circumstances totally changed rather than slightly improved. Many
people are agreed that priority should be given to reuniting
these broken families, but the only way to do that, when dealing
with a community that is ninety per cent agriculturist, is to
resettle them on spare land in some remote region of the world
—which, as Tibetans can endure more hardship than most,
should not be impossible. If only someone would take up the
project of moving them *en masse* to a suitable area they could

then be left alone to get on with the job in their own way—
minus the Red Cross, C.R.C., C.A.R.E., S.A.T., A.E.R.,
C.U.S.O., W.C.C., S.C.F., S.C.I., and etc., etc. Obviously
there would be tremendous legal and political obstacles in the
way of implementing such a scheme. Yet surely it's worth trying, not merely because it would finally solve the practical
problem of caring for these people but also because it would
give them a reasonable chance to preserve their culture.
Rumours are current that one such project was recently mooted
but promptly quashed by the Tibetan authorities on the
grounds that for Tibetans to move *en masse* to a more distant
country would be an overt abandonment of all hope of returning to Tibet.


31 AUGUST

To-day Namgyal left for Switzerland with Thondup, his son—
or nephew, as the case may be. He had worked in the Dispensary as general factotum for eighteen months and we were
sad to see him go; but he has been longing to set sail, or take
wing, to the 'Paradise' of Europe, where he is convinced that his
son will prosper automatically, by the mere fact of being in the
West.

His story is rather an unusual one. He was the youngest of
the three husbands of an apparently not very kindly wife, who
treated him as a house-boy rather than as a husband, so when
the exodus to India began he chose the child most likely to be
his own and quietly departed from the village of Gombol.
(Don't ask me where Gombol is; Tibetans measure distances
in their own way and Thondup simply said that it was 'one
month's walk from Lhasa over the Mountain of the Wind-God'
—which is not a very precise indication of the spot.) Having
been at school in Mussoorie, Thondup—now aged twelve—
speaks adequate English; he is a delightful boy, but as usual I
have horrible misgivings about the impact of Europe on a
Tiblet.

During the past year Namgyal and one of the ayahs have
been living together and I must say that their recent demeanour
belies what I wrote some time ago about the emotional lives of

Tibetans. It's been most distressing to see the two of them sitting silently outside the Dispensary whenever they had a free moment, holding hands and looking like Rodin statues of Sorrow—as if both hadn't had enough upheavals in their lives already. The ayah naturally wanted to go to Switzerland too, but the Powers who arrange such things seem quite insensitive to refugees as individuals—so many males and so many females are transported from Point A to Point B without any attempt being made to cater for contingencies such as this. One has to admire Namgyal for sacrificing his own happiness to give Thondup the 'benefit' of a European education.

## 2 SEPTEMBER

I woke this morning with mumps, an infection taken no more seriously around here than is a head-cold in Ireland: every week an ayah or a few children develop it—but they wouldn't dream of calling *that* an illness and carry on regardless. Irishwomen, however, are of inferior mettle, so after breakfast I shamelessly took to my bed—or rather to the wooden Tibetan couch on which Kesang sleeps at night, since I haven't got a bed proper. My eyes have been troublesome lately, and now Oliver thinks I've got a touch of trachoma—which is not surprising, as the majority of the children suffer severely from this infection. He has advised me not to read or write for a week, which fits in quite well with being mumpsical; I feel no great urge to do anything more than pity myself this evening. Yet you can't really resent a disease called mumps—it's such a *jolly* word!

## 9 SEPTEMBER

Mumps abated, eyes improved and back to work to-day. This morning a messenger came to the Dispensary from Mrs Tsiring Dolma's office at the Upper Nursery and said that she had issued an order forbidding the taking of photographs in the camp by any Westerners who had not first obtained her permission to use a camera. We were understandably enraged—no one but the Indian Government or Military Authorities has the legal right to impose such a restriction and I at once sent to

Lower Dharamsala for three rolls of film. This is the sort of thing that repeatedly happens to upset relations when you've been trying hard to feel fraternal charity towards the lady in question. Granted it's always possible in Tibland that things are not what they seem—this order *could* have emanated from the Indian Authorities, who may have their own reasons for not wishing the outside world to see just how grim conditions are here. In such a case Mrs Tsiring Dolma, as a face-saving measure, might well represent the order to be her own.

We heard at lunch-time that yesterday evening a policeman from Lower Dharamsala was killed by a bear in the forest near His Holiness's Palace. The dangerous thing is to meet one face to face on a winding mountain path; then they are terrified and attack, but if they hear your approach they will always run away. So you are advised to sing loudly when walking alone on such paths and, should the worst happen while you are briefly resting the larynx, you are recommended to lie down at once and remain quite still; apparently an upright human has a most deleterious effect on a bear's nervous system. Personally I should have thought that lying quite still in the shadow of a jittery bear would have an even more deleterious effect on a human's nervous system. But the point has been noted.

## 10 September

This is evidently a very inauspicious date. To begin with poor Oliver has caught the mumps and is in a most pathetic panic, foreseeing the end of the Senn dynasty. Then this afternoon one of the ayahs, who eleven days ago was safely delivered of her third baby in Kangra Hospital, returned here seriously ill. It's an incredible story. Rinchin was aged twenty-four and Dubkay, our thirty-year-old junior teacher, was her second husband. (Her first, the father of two elder children, did not escape from Tibet with his family.) About six weeks ago she came to the Dispensary and told Oliver that soon after the baby's birth she would die, though the child would be perfectly healthy. Oliver examined her thoroughly and said: 'Nonsense! You've nothing to worry about and your baby will need you so don't think of such a thing any more.' However, as she was slightly anaemic he took the precaution of advising her to go to the Kangra Hospital for the confinement. At first she refused to consider this, repeating that she *knew* she was going to die and that she wished to be at Dharamsala, near His Holiness, when the time came. Oliver again reassured her but could see that he was making no impression. He then got Dubkay to persuade her to go to hospital, and twelve days ago she, Dubkay and Dubkay's aunt (a nun) all left for Kangra. (Until her labour pains came on she had continued to do her normal daily work and to look perfectly healthy.) On 30 August she was easily delivered of a fine son weighing five and a quarter pounds and for the next week mother and child did well. Then, three days ago, she suddenly announced that she couldn't walk any more (though she'd been up every day and had even gone to the bazaar with Dubkay one afternoon), that she couldn't eat and that she wished to return immediately to Dharamsala to die. Dr Haslem tried everything she knew, but could make no satisfactory diagnosis much less prescribe a cure, so this morning when Rinchin insisted on moving back to the camp there seemed no point in opposing her wish.

After her arrival here no one told us how ill she was; apparently all concerned accepted the fact that she must inevitably die unless the Lamas could exorcise the death-demon which had taken possession of her. It is significant that in this major health crisis the assistance of trained Western medical helpers was not even considered—despite the many proofs of the efficiency of modern medicine given to the Tibetans in this area. Like the Celts of pre-Christian Europe the Tibetans believe that death is never natural, but is always caused by the evil influence of one of the many types of death-demon. And presumably in the case of a young, outwardly healthy person the demon responsible is held to be exceptionally powerful and evil.

So it was by chance that Juliet discovered the position, when she noticed two of the dispensary ayahs whispering and weeping and looking frightened. They rather reluctantly told her what was wrong and she and I immediately went up to the little stone hut on the mountain-side above the camp, where Dubkay and his wife had their home. (By now Oliver was running a temperature and couldn't leave his bed.)

Dubkay was sitting on the edge of the charpoy holding his wife in his arms, stroking her hair gently and weeping. In another corner of the tiny room his aunt was inexpertly preparing a bottle-feed for the infant, who lay concealed in a bundle of dirty rags, and the remaining floor-space was occupied by standing ayahs who argued and sobbed in the intervals between gazing silently at the dying woman with a sort of fascinated terror.

We saw at once that she *was* dying, though she seemed fully conscious. A brief examination showed that her heart was failing, so Juliet proposed that she should be given an injection to stimulate it. To this Dubkay agreed, though in a manner suggesting that he was merely pandering to our whims: but when he translated the proposal to the ayahs they protested violently. However, Juliet then sent me to fetch what was needed from the Dispensary.

When I returned most of the ayahs had gone and His Holiness's personal physician, attended by a Lama, had just arrived from the Palace. The 'am-chi' felt the patient's pulse at wrist and ankle, laid his ear for a moment on the abdomen and then, murmuring something to Dubkay, withdrew to allow the Lama to perform the necessary rites. An ayah had brought a saucepan of glowing wood-embers from the kitchen and on these incense was sprinkled and the saucepan handed to Dubkay, who held it close to his wife's face, while the Lama wafted the smoke towards her nostrils. I couldn't decide whether this was in fact a religious rite or simply a form of smelling-salts. One of the English interpreters from the Palace had now joined us, but though I questioned him on various points he obviously did not wish to discuss the religious aspect of the scene with an outsider. He merely mentioned that for the past few months Rinchin had been having terrifyingly vivid nightmares about the present condition of her family in Tibet, where she had left her parents, her husband, a sister and three young brothers. Seemingly she and the two children had been alone in their home in Lhasa when the Uprising took place and for the children's sakes she had immediately fled, but had ever since regretted not having waited—either to help the rest of the family to escape or to face the Chinese repression with them.

F

Suddenly the incense—or something else—took effect and Rinchin, who had been reclining against a bed-roll, sat bolt upright without assistance and began to talk in a low but very clear voice. At once the ayahs, who had by now reassembled, stopped their agitated chattering and seemed hardly to breathe. Rinchin spoke emphatically for four or five minutes, appearing perfectly lucid, and then lay back again. Without looking directly at anyone I could feel the fear in the room—it almost amounted to mass-hysteria—and for the first and only time in my life I experienced that sensation known as 'hair prickling on the back of the neck'.

I whispered an enquiry to the interpreter and he replied briefly that Rinchin had described her visions and concluded by affirming that a few months ago an Evil Spirit from Tibet had entered into her and she had known then that after the birth she would die.

Now the Lama anointed Rinchin's ears, eyes and nose with butter-fat, before going into a trance to attempt to exorcise the Evil Spirit. Within moments he had gone completely rigid as he sat cross-legged, his eyes open but blank and beads of sweat standing out on his face. By this time Juliet had taken the unfortunate baby to our bungalow for a feed and I was left distributing brandy by the spoonful to Rinchin, Dubkay—and myself. Soon the Lama had gone so white and was sweating so hard and looking so odd that I feared he might die first. Two other Lamas now arrived, carrying the *Bardo Thödol* (a Tibetan Buddhist scripture recited for the benefit of the dying and the dead) rolled up in two silver cylinders. These manuscripts were immediately unfolded and the monks began to chant them *sotto voce* in that indescribable Tibetan manner which has to be heard to be believed. At this point, since I could do no more for either Rinchin or Dubkay, I left the hut and hurried down the dark mountain-side to the bungalow, telling myself that I was hurrying because of bears and that it was absolutely ridiculous to think in terms of death-demons.

An hour later the interpreter came to tell us that Rinchin was dead.

I haven't been feeling very energetic to-day. Last night, after diary-writing, Rinchin's death prompted me to continue my study of Dr Evans-Wentz' edition of the *Bardo Thödol*—which in the circumstances made such absorbing reading that it was 2.30 a.m. before I put out the light.

This must be one of the world's most remarkable books. Tradition says that it was compiled during the early centuries of Lamaism—if not actually during the lifetime of Padma Sambhava himself—and to the average reader it certainly gives the impression of having been strongly influenced by the old animist Bön-Po religion. However, Lama Anagorika Govinda points out that it cannot be regarded as propagating Bön ideas, since it firmly declares its adherence to Padma Sambhava, the man responsible for replacing Bönism by Buddhism. Therefore the Bön influence should be interpreted not as a dilution of the original Buddhist doctrine, but as the consequence of Padma Sambhava's compromise with the local Tibetan deities, whom he appointed as guardians of the new faith. Bönism did have a crude doctrine of rebirth, yet, from what little else is known of it, there were few other points of contact with Buddhism, so this 'appointment' of its gods must have been an expedient manœuvre to reconcile the more fanatical followers of the old faith to the new. Such a manœuvre was permissible within the framework of orthodox Buddhism, which has always tolerated the reverencing of the gods of earth and space, as guardians of the 'Dharma'. Yet it is probably true to say that Lamaism, as practised by uneducated lay-people, retains a stronger animist element than any other Buddhist School—particularly, it seems, among the Gelug-pa sect, which might be described as the State Church of Tibet. This is an odd circumstance, because the Gelug-pas (also known as the 'Yellow-Hats' and 'The Virtuous') are in fact the Reformed Church, established by Tsong-Kapa in the late fourteenth century, and one would have assumed them to be least influenced by the ancient religion. However, there was no reason to fear the rivalry of Bönism by that date, when the surviving Bön-pos had completed the process of so closely remodelling their religion on Buddhist lines that outsiders found it difficult to distinguish between the two iconographies and literatures. Therefore the Gelug-pas could in turn borrow from the Bön-pos without loss of dignity and they chose to reintroduce one of the most powerful Bönist institutions—the State Oracles. Oracle-Temples are now to be found in most Yellow Sect Monasteries and the deities invoked therein are exclusively Bönist.

The Bön-pos, like most other primitive people, had their rituals for the benefit and guidance of the dead, but the *Bardo Thödol*, though incorporating some of these, presents far more complex theories about Life, Death and Rebirth than could have been evolved by a people without any literature of their own. It belongs to the same eschatological tradition as Plato's *Tenth Book of the Republic*, the Egyptian *Book of the Dead* and the medieval *Ars Moricado*. Sir John Woodroffe has described it as a 'Traveller's Guide to Other Worlds', since it recounts, with a considerable knowledge of depth psychology, the experiences of the deceased between death and rebirth. But it can also provide the means of comforting and strengthening those who are on their death-bed and, most important of all, its essential teaching is intended to be assimilated and acted on throughout life, so that the Buddhist ideal of meeting death serenely, lucidly and bravely may be realized when the time comes. In our age the Tibetans are unique as the only people to study the Art of Dying as something equalling in importance the Art of Living. This is a corollary to their belief that ' . . . the last thought at the moment of death determines the character of the next incarnation'—a theory recalling the Hebrew teaching, 'As a man thinketh in his heart, so is he.'

However, yesterday's recitation of the *Bardo Thödol* was merely an example of the popular use to which the book is now put by the majority who, misunderstanding its purpose, use it thus in the belief that such a recitation will effect the 'liberation' of the dying person from the cycle of birth and rebirth. One can hardly blame the ordinary monks and lay-people for their superstitious misinterpretations and debasements of the Buddhist doctrine, considering how few people have been admitted throughout the centuries to the circle of initiates. In this respect Southern Buddhist criticisms of Northern Buddhism, as a type of gnosticism and a deviation from the Pali Canon, seem justified.

In his introduction to *The Tibetan Book of the Dead*, as the English translation of the *Bardo Thödol* is entitled, Dr Evans-Wentz makes a very interesting comparison between the Bible, the Koran and the *Bardo Thödol*. He observes that whereas the former two books present, as real events, those spiritual experiences which take the form of visions or hallucinations, the *Bardo Thödol* presents them as purely illusionary and symbolic, thereby revealing a much deeper understanding of the human mind than was common in earlier centuries. Yet here again we see the disparity between the esoteric and exoteric interpretations; many now regard these symbolic descriptions of after-death experiences just as credulously as we regarded the Bible two hundred years ago.

Dr Evans-Wentz also remarks on the link between the Tibetan doctrine of rebirth and 'the purgatorial lore now Christianized and associated with St Patrick's Purgatory in Ireland, and the whole cycle of Otherworld and Rebirth legends of the Celtic peoples connected with their Fairy-Faith'. In his book* Dr Evans-Wentz has suggested that this purgatorial lore, which was centred about a cavern for mystic pagan initiations on an island in Lough Derg, may have inspired the doctrine of Purgatory in the Catholic Church. He mentions that the original cavern was demolished by order of the British Government, in an attempt to destroy pagan superstition. According to Tibetan eschatology rebirth in this world is the equivalent of the Catholic Purgatory and is the normal person's lot. Only the exceptionally evil man is condemned to Hell and only the exceptionally good man attains Nirvana.

When Juliet went back to the hut last night, after being told of Rinchin's death, she found it already deserted by everyone except a Lama and she had to return here to find the unhappy Dubkay, who was so crazed with grief that it required two men to hold him down and prevent him from injuring himself. Juliet gave him a sedative which soon sent him to sleep, but

* *Fairy Faith in Celtic Countries* (Oxford, 1911).

everyone else seemed to remain awake, and all night we could hear women wailing and men beating drums to frighten off the Evil Spirit.

The Tibetan custom is to throw a white cloth over the corpse's face as soon as death takes place and nobody is allowed to touch the deceased while the complete separation of soul from body is believed to be in progress. This takes from three and a half to four days, unless hastened by a priest known as the *hpho-bo* or 'extractor of the consciousness principle'. But even with the *hpho-bo's* assistance it is held that the deceased is not aware of separation from the body until this period has passed. In Rinchin's case a *hpho-bo* came immediately and he was the Lama seen sitting at the head of the corpse by Juliet.

The *hpho-bo* usually dismisses everyone from the death-chamber and has all the doors and windows sealed to ensure the silence necessary for the performance of his ritual. Next he intones a mystic chant and, after ordering the spirit to detach itself from living relatives and material goods and to leave the body, he scrutinizes the crown of the head at the sagittal suture, known as the 'Aperture of Brahma', and if the scalp is not bald removes a few hairs from immediately over the aperture.

While this ceremony is being conducted a *tsi-pa* or astrologer-Lama, is elsewhere casting a horoscope to discover who may approach and handle the corpse, how and when it should be disposed of and what rites should be performed to assist the deceased—this depending on the precise nature of the death-demon concerned. Next the corpse is arranged in a sitting position, known as the 'embryonic posture', and is placed in one corner of the room. When I went up to the hut this morning Rinchin was arranged thus and two Lamas were reciting the *Bardo Thödol*. A bowl of food stood before the corpse, for it is customary to offer the deceased a share of each meal eaten by the family and by visiting mourners between the times of death and burial. Similarly, during the forty-nine-day period which is believed to elapse between death and rebirth, an effigy of the corpse is kept in the corner of the room formerly occupied by the deceased and is regularly offered food. This effigy is made by dressing some suitable object such as a stool in the dead person's clothes and inserting a printed paper where the face should be. On this the inscription reads: 'I, the world's depart-ing one, (name), adore and take refuge in my Lama-confessor, and all the deities, both mild and wrathful; and may "the Great Pitier" forgive my accumulated sins and impurities of former lives and show me the way to another good world.'

Dr Evans-Wentz finds the use of this effigy 'So definitely akin to the effigy of the deceased called "the Statue of the Osiris", as used in the funeral rites of Ancient Egypt, as to suggest a common origin.' And Dr L. A. Waddell writes: 'This is essenti-ally a Bön rite, and is referred to as such in the histories of Guru Padma Sambhava, as having been practised by the Bön, and as having incurred the displeasure of the founder of Lamaism.' It is rather characteristic of the Tibetans that while doctrines come and go they quietly but firmly adhere to the rites that please them.

We were told this evening that the astrologer had declared 4 a.m. to-morrow to be an auspicious time for the funeral. Then, every week until the forty-nine days are over, Lamas will come to the hut to read the *Bardo Thödol*. At the end of this period the effigy's face-paper is 'ceremoniously burned in the flame of a butter-lamp and the spirit of the deceased given a final fare-well', its fate being deduced from the colour of the burning paper and the way in which the flame behaves. Next the effigy is taken apart and the clothes given to the Lamas, who sell them as part of their fee. A year later a feast is held in honour of the deceased and after this the widow or widower is at liberty to marry again.

Having no standard of comparison I wouldn't know whether the death ceremonies performed here to-day were simple or elaborate. They looked elaborate, but in view of Dubkay's financial standing were probably simple—only two Lamas are reciting the *Bardo Thödol* in the hut, whereas a rich man would have up to a hundred Lamas chanting in his home or in the temple where the deceased usually worshipped.

This morning, when I went on my 'ear-rounds', I saw that one of the girls' rooms had been taken over by the Lamas and converted to a little temple, where ceremonies continued all day. Another small altar-table was set up on the veranda of our bungalow, and here three of the saintliest-looking old Lamas

I've ever seen sat cross-legged for hours, performing strange rites with the butter-lamps, little bowls of foodstuffs and 'tormas' (sacrificial cakes) arranged on the altar before them. I longed to stop and examine everything closely but, not wishing to display an outsider's vulgar curiosity during such solemn rites, I had to be content with casual glimpses obtained while passing. These were enough to reveal the very great beauty of the silver ceremonial vessels, and later this evening I learned that most of these are four or five hundred years old.

Juliet's first job to-day was to look for a wet-nurse for Dubkay's baby—provisionally named Sonam Nobo, which means 'Lucky Precious Thing'. But in this respect he was not lucky. Many of the ayahs are feeding babies and normally they vie with one another to take on any waif or stray; yet, though expressing endless sympathy for both father and son, they all had an excuse why Sonam Nobo could not be nursed. Rinchin's death-demon is still very much among those present and Kesang admitted to me that the ayahs believed it might now have entered into the baby—despite Rinchin's certainty that her child would be safe. So, as it is out of the question to entrust Tibetans with bottle-feeding, Sonam Nobo remains in our bungalow, sleeping between us in a Tibetan table turned upside down (Tibetan tables are virtually boxes, some 2′ 6″ high) and doing nicely, thank you. He requires sustenance half-hourly, as far as I can see—or hear—but since I'm terrified of such microscopic humans Juliet has absolved me from my share of the responsibility and she and Kesang will cope between them.

This evening, just after Juliet had left the camp to escort a bad asthma case to Kangra Hospital, Dubkay called to see his son. Never have I witnessed such a pathetic scene. He burst into tears the moment I lifted the tiny object out of its box— but somehow in this environment there's nothing odd or embarrassing about a man in tears—and then he sat on the floor for over an hour, cuddling and kissing the infant so incessantly that I thought he'd suffocate it. The only thing that stopped his quiet sobbing was the sight of Sonam Nobo yawning—an operation which made Dubkay beam all over his face. Occasionally he'd look up and proudly draw my attention to the fact that the prodigy's finger-nails were growing or that its hair was thinning—he hasn't yet got adjusted to the whole mysterious business of being father to a real live son!

When Dubkay had left Kesang came in, at the conclusion of the ayahs' night-prayers, and I remarked to her how sad it was to see Dubkay's grief, but how fortunate that he had Sonam Nobo to console him. Kesang agreed and added revealingly—'Dubkay and Rinchin were very good friends. He says he can easily get another wife and in one year will surely be married again. But he says he knows he will never have another friend like Rinchin.'

## 12 SEPTEMBER

Walking down to the Dispensary at 5.30 this morning we saw eerie evidence of the funeral, and in the grey early light I found myself shivering slightly—one doesn't have to be very suggestible to react to the intensity of the camp's present atmosphere.

En route from the hut to the burning-ghat by the river every single road, path, track and doorway was 'sealed off' against the Evil Spirit by a six-inch-wide line of white flour, which at one point extended for twenty yards across the compound. The road to Dall Lake, on one's right leaving the compound, had its line, as had the tracks to the Upper Nursery, to the Dispensary, to Forsythe Bazaar and to the Military Cantonment down the mountain-side. Only the road to the river was 'open'.

I didn't hear the funeral moving off, but Juliet was up at 4 a.m., feeding Sonam Nobo, and heard the chanting of the Lamas, the beating of hand-drums, the clashing of brass cymbals and the blowing of human thigh-bone trumpets and sacred conch-shells. The cremation itself must have been quite a brief ceremony for on our return to breakfast we found a tearful Dubkay squatting in the corner fondling Sonam Nobo.

The Lamas again had an active time to-day as they continued their exorcizing campaign by swinging censers of delightful incense in every corner of every room in the camp. Three of them also prayed for an hour in our room, giving Sonam Nobo innumerable blessings. But they won't hold the 'Naming Blessing Ceremony' for another month.

## 4

# Difficulties and Diversions

To-day twenty-eight Tiblets were transferred from the Lower to the Upper Nursery—a gratuitously unfeeling action on the part of the camp authorities. Not that it's entirely their fault: the woolly bureaucracy of Tibland in general is also evident here.

There's a transit camp at Lower Dharamsala where forty-seven children in the eight-to-fourteen age-group are now living in the most appalling squalor—without ayahs, medical care, blankets, mugs, spoons, drinkable water or anything else. This establishment is supervised by one of the corrupt Tibetans—and a corrupt Tibetan is as astonishingly bad as an incorrupt Tibetan is astonishingly good. If one of the relief agencies sends supplies and equipment—as they occasionally do, following an inspection by some shocked foreigner—these are normally flogged in the local bazaars within a week of their arrival. The present group of children have now been at Lower Dharamsala for five months (it all depends on what you mean by 'transit'!) and it's anybody's guess when they will be moved elsewhere. So my argument is that when children are sent from the Upper Nursery to the Mussoorie Schools these unfortunates from Lower Dharamsala should replace them. This would both ease the situation at the transit camp and avoid separating our lot from the ayahs they've grown to love and depend on *in loco parentis*. But no—the transit camp is technically a 'school' (the fact that it has no teacher is apparently irrelevant), whereas the Upper Nursery is not a 'school' (though Doris and two Tibetan teachers are available) so the Indian authorities would not approve of such a transfer. Sometimes one finds one's patience wearing a little thin in Tibland.

Actually my patience evaporated completely this afternoon when Mr Phalla—Mrs Tsiring Dolma's second-in-command—

came to choose the twenty-eight. We are never given any warning of such events and as I was de-worming 108 Tiblets, having just expended an enormous amount of nervous energy on sorting them out from among the other hundreds, Mr Phalla came rushing into the room waving the long sleeves of his robe and looking like a demented ostrich. He shouted a few Tibetan phrases and before I could intervene my precious 108 tape-worm cases had vanished. Swearing, I shot out after them, to see every child in the camp lined up on the compound with half a dozen clerks from the office scuttling up and down the lines, picking out one here and one there. Ten minutes later it was all over and the lines had broken up and there were little groups of ayahs and children clinging to each other and weeping their eyes out. There was also me, still swearing as I darted round clutching my list of tape-worm numbers and peering at the (usually wrong) numbers around hundreds of necks. As if life wasn't difficult enough already for all concerned.

To-day's sensation arrived at 5.30 p.m. in the very shapely shape of a twenty-five-year-old Indian nurse appointed by the Punjab Government to work here for three years. Juliet, Oliver and I just stood with our mouths open when she announced herself; it's typical of Tibland that no one in the camp had known of her appointment until that moment. Naturally enough she wanted somewhere to sleep so we cheerfully offered the usual floor in our bungalow, on which all casual Western visitors to the camp are of necessity accommodated. But Sister Sawnay raised her eyebrows slightly at this and said that she had meant a *bed*. We said, 'Sorry, no-can-do,' so she promptly returned to Lower Dharamsala to say the Hindi equivalent of 'What the Hell!' to the Local Government Authorities. But I should think she'll be back, as she must need the job, having left a husband and a two-year-old daughter in Delhi. Her husband is also a nurse and Juliet tells me that there are more male than female nurses in India. Sister Sawnay earns £10 a month and her husband earns between £12 and £13—which seems very little indeed considering the high cost of living in present-day India.

A few days ago a rather tiresome American woman visited the camp, and in the course of her—fortunately brief—stay accused me of 'romancing' about the exceptional qualities of Tiblets. I rapidly lost my temper, picked up Spencer Chapman's *Lhasa: The Holy City* and in a triumphant tone read out his comments on Tibetan children:

> We were much struck to see how charmingly they behaved to each other; when one boy spilt his curry into his lap [at a children's party] the others laughed with him—not at him—and helped to clear it up. The small children never seem to cry and without ever being fussed by their parents they behave perfectly. A Tibetan mother never says 'Don't', yet the child doesn't.

My critic was more subdued after that; it's very useful to be able to quote an expert in support of one's own observations.


21 SEPTEMBER

To-day the whole camp was thoroughly disorganized because His Holiness had ordered three sessions of special prayers to be said for the Buddhists in South Vietnam. At the most disconcerting moments all the staff drop everything to pray, and as we sat hopefully waiting for our lunch to appear we heard them beginning half an hour's chanting of hymns!

By now Dubkay has become almost resident in our bungalow. He sits for hours in a corner talking to his 'pooh'—and I'm convinced that Sonam Nobo knows him already. Personally I find month-old human infants singularly unattractive, but Dubkay obviously couldn't agree less. He brings the 'pooh' a little gift almost every day and seems to have abandoned his job—I fail to see what time can be left for teaching between visits to the son and heir.

This morning I chanced to observe Tibetan school-discipline in action. Because four little boys had treated a Holy Scarf disrespectfully they were made to stand in front of the class, bent double, holding their left ear forward with their right hands and vice versa—a posture which had to be maintained without a break for about fifteen minutes. Of course corporal punishment as we know it is unheard of here—but this punishment looks exceedingly uncomfortable, if not painful.

It is noticeable that Tiblets have no scruples about 'sneaking'. To-day the teacher merely asked the class which of them had thrown the scarf over the rafters and at once the four culprits were pointed out by everyone else. Yet after the punishment period the quartet smilingly rejoined their 'betrayers' and the whole process was completely taken for granted by all. The class hadn't 'told on them' out of any spite or enmity, but simply because this is the tradition, and the culprits bore no grudge. I must admit that we find this tradition most convenient in our daily efforts to cope with so many children. We have strictly forbidden the use, as toys, of little glass bottles or nails, yet often the tiniest acquire these and won't willingly part with them so, if an older child spots this breach of the regulations, he'll report it to one of us. I often wonder why the 'seniors' don't themselves take these dangerous objects from the 'juniors' but seemingly this doesn't occur to them. Possibly the explanation is that a certain amount of force would be required to remove a beloved bottle from the clenched fist of a two-year-old and Tiblets are conditioned not to use force. Certainly our ban on such playthings is fully justified. The other morning in the Dispensary my blood froze when a three-year-old opened her mouth and casually removed from it a piece of broken glass in order to make way for her quota of pills.

However, though we appreciate the Tibetan lack of 'esprit de corps' when dealing with children, we do find that when dealing with adults it can on occasions make life intolerably complicated. In fact such a basic ethical difference probably creates the widest and deepest gulf between our two civilizations; only when living in a society where no such principles of loyalty exist does one begin to appreciate the extent to which our reactions, attitudes and instinctive behaviour are based on the schoolboy commandment: 'Thou shalt not sneak.' It's not for me to pronounce on the relative merits of the two codes— probably the Western, if abused, can have as disintegrating an effect as the Tibetan does—but to be suddenly in a world where something so fundamental to us doesn't operate can often take one completely out of one's depth in both personal relations and business matters.

It's now 11 p.m. but Kesang has not yet come in, which

means that a story-telling session is in progress. This telling of epic tales is one of the favourite adult recreations and three of the ayahs are experts. Often it takes three or four nights to complete a story, beginning each session after prayers and finishing about midnight. I went out one evening to watch and saw every man and woman in the camp sitting around the ayah who was recounting the epic, listening so intently that they did not even notice my presence. The 'Seanchaí', as we would call her in Ireland, was using a wooden box as 'platform', so that all could see her gestures, and was telling her tale with great verve and expression. She must have felt quite exhausted after continuing thus for almost four hours.

Sister Sawnay has now got a room in Macleod Ganj and every morning she comes by bus to Forsythe Bazaar and then walks up the very steep quarter-mile path to the Nursery—a 'marathon' which, being a typical city girl, she regards with horror. I innocently asked her why she didn't walk by the mile-long Top Road, instead of taking the bus along the two-mile Low Road, but she shrank from the mere thought of walking a mile every morning and said that if she attempted such a feat she'd be too tired to do anything else all day.

The weather during this past week has been perfection—pleasantly hot sun, a slight, fresh breeze and the whole world vigorously green after the monsoon. Here, at this season, one feels simultaneously the freshness of spring and the melancholy of autumn: but of course there will be no riot of changing leaves as these forests are not deciduous.

We're trying to get the children to sunbathe as therapy for their skin diseases—but Tibetans are allergic to hot sun so it's not being a very successful campaign. On Sunday last I decided after lunch to sunbathe for half an hour, and I hadn't been stretched out on a little patch of grass for more than two minutes when Cama Yishy came along, hurrying as best he could under the enormous weight of an open umbrella. This he carefully placed over me so that only my legs were exposed to the lethal rays. Then he beamed as if to say, 'That's better, isn't it?' and sat himself down in the shade beside my head.

I've just noticed something interesting. A few moments ago

an ant was crawling up my left arm and quite automatically I blew it off and it continued its crawl across the floor. Only then did I register the fact that three months ago I'd have just as automatically squashed it to death. I've not consciously acquired any new principles about preserving life so it must simply be the effect of living in such a highly concentrated Buddhist atmosphere. It was the spontaneity of the action that struck me as so significant.

## THE 11TH DAY OF THE 8TH MONTH OF THE WATER-HARE YEAR

Admittedly this date doesn't sound probable, but it is literally the Tibetan equivalent of 28 September 1963. And 1962 was the Water-Tiger Year, and 1964 will be the Wood-Dragon Year—enchanting! But the Water-Hare particularly takes my fancy: it could be out of *Alice*!

Last night was quite cold with a slight gale blowing and this morning the rugged peaks above us were smooth and radiant with new snow after the first blizzard of the winter. This afternoon I had a job to do in the Upper Nursery, and when walking back via Dall Lake—now rapidly shrinking—I saw hundreds of monkeys coming down to their winter quarters in the warmth of the Kangra valley. These dainty, delightful creatures are very curious and unafraid—unless you point a camera at them, when they flee, mistaking it for a gun. The babies are specially lovable, as they sit staring wide-eyed at this strange cousin who returns their fascinated wonder with interest! After seeing them playing tip-and-tig in the freedom of towering green trees I could never again visit a zoo and look at their captured brothers listlessly climbing dead branches and wearing sad, patchy coats.

The Tibetans are celebrating some special feast to-day, and 'tormas' were very much in evidence. These conical-shaped sacrificial cakes are believed to be the Lamaist substitute for the human and animal sacrifices of the Bön-pos, and apart from their use as temple offerings they are also eaten on special occasions. The basic ingredients are barley-flour, butter and water and they are coloured dark brown, so that at first sight they look like some attractive chocolate confection—but appearances can indeed be deceptive. This morning Chumba honoured us by bringing a 'torma' to Juliet and me for our exclusive enjoyment. It was presented on a large platter, and around the base were strewn nuts and slices of raw onion and gaudy boiled sweets and slivers of cheese and dirty sultanas. Proudly laying this gift on the breakfast table Chumba stood waiting for us to sample it and go into a gastronomic ecstasy, so there was no alternative but to carve it up and feign delight— what an effort! No one can accuse me of being faddy about food but I really thought my stomach would instantly reject this hideous concoction and ever since it's been haunting me. It felt like sticky, gritty clay in the mouth and it tasted like poison. Yet Tibetans revel in the stuff, and all day the children have been going around clutching and sucking wedges of it—as I know to my cost, since by evening I was covered in the mixture. Naturally possession of it does not diminish their affection and they hug and caress you none the less enthusiastically for having this sordid mess in their fists.

Sometimes, observing how Tiblets treat food, I marvel that the camp's diseases aren't even more numerous and deadly. One sees bits of moo-moo or potato that have been saved from a meal being carried around for hours inside the clothes next the skin, then falling into one of the channels that run through the compound, serving as latrines at night, and then being retrieved and eaten with relish. And if the Tiblet in question is too small to fish it out of the channel for himself an ayah will come rushing along and return the tidbit to its owner with a fond smile. Another of the ayahs' startling habits is to feed very small Tiblets, who may be ill and disinclined to drink, by filling their own mouths with liquid and transferring this to the patient's mouth. Recently I observed an ayah with mumps thus treating a year-old baby.

It's pathetic to see how the children, despite being forced to wear Western clothes, insist on carrying their few possessions in Tibetan style. Even when a Western garment has pockets they ignore these and improvise Tibetan pouches above the waist by tying something very tightly around their middles—how they survive this constriction is beyond my comprehension.

Himalayan farm

Tibetan camp

Pooh-Bah disposes of a chapatti
Fingers are useful for scraping out mugs
Suppertime while the sun is still warm

## 29 SEPTEMBER

To-day, being Sunday, I'll take the opportunity to introduce you to Pooh-Bah. (Perhaps his name should be spelt 'Puba'— but the temptation is irresistible!) This three-year-old effort-lessly dominates the camp, though in physical stature he is the smallest object outside the Babies' Room; everyone adores him, and any child-psychologist would go grey overnight at the irresponsible adulation and pandering to which he is exposed. For no apparent reason, except that he is Pooh-Bah, a special ayah personally attends him. He should be in Room Six with the three- and four-year-olds, but as this accommodation is rather gloomy, with more than its share of bed-bugs, he has chosen Room Two which leaks badly yet has a delightful out-look. And here he lords it over one hundred eight- and nine-year-olds.

Pooh-Bah is the most beautiful child in the camp. His features are meltingly cherubic and the knowledge that in this case appearances deceive adds piquancy to the large, liquid brown eyes with their long, upsweeping lashes, and to the round, golden-tanned face, complete with dimples and slightly pursed lips. When one analyses Pooh-Bah's character a number of unpleasant and very un-Tibetan traits are soon discovered— but somehow one doesn't often stop to analyse it because the little wretch possesses more charm to the cubic inch than any other child in the place.

He is aggressive yet this is readily forgiven, since those he attacks are always considerably larger than himself. Tibetans are not bred to fight back so it is a common occurrence to hear howls of agony from some corner of the compound and then to find Pooh-Bah sitting on a prone eight-year-old's back, sadistic-ally pounding his victim's head with an empty pill bottle. He accepts adult intervention with a good grace and even permits a certain amount of consolation to the afflicted, but if he judges that the situation is getting out of control, and that he himself is in danger of being forgotten, he will take your hand and with an imperious gesture convey that enough is enough.

He is also a hypochondriac, and diseases taken for granted by the other children are a source of absorbing interest to him.

His scabies, his rotten teeth, his worms, his dysentery, his trachoma, his bronchitis, his otitis media—all are cunningly used to excite the sympathy and generosity of the camp, as though he alone were suffering. But his greatest pride and joy was a cut forehead, adorned by three stitches. This, being exclusive to Pooh-Bah, was shown individually to every member of the camp, and one frequently saw people being solemnly led by the hand on a sort of pilgrimage to the Scene of the Accident, where the martyr would explain just how he fell off the table and acquired this grievous wound. Yet his is not a morbid personality, though—again unlike the average Tiblet—he rarely smiles. But when he does the smile is of such a ravishing sweetness that everyone privileged to come within its radius feels that their day has been made.

Normally, however, Pooh-Bah expresses his good humour by singing an interminable solo—and in this at least he is a true Tibetan. Not being gregarious he saunters alone around the compound, occasionally pausing by a group of children to consider their activities. Then, if a musical mood comes upon him, he wanders off to the edge of the compound to sing his song while gazing down on the Kangra valley 4,000 feet below —with his little pot-belly almost protruding over the precipice.

Undisguised greed is another of Pooh-Bah's failings, and this is indeed unique among Tiblets, who so often share with their room-mates whatever few delicacies happen to come their way. Pooh-Bah's delicacies, however, are neither few nor shared. At every hour of the day he may be seen clutching some biscuit or sweet or piece of cheese, and instead of discreetly consuming these ill-gotten gains in a quiet corner he struts up and down loudly sucking, or sits at some prominent vantage point conspicuously munching. By all the laws of human nature he should be universally detested on this count alone.

Inevitably, Pooh-Bah has first pick from the clothing gift-parcels and he is at the moment attired in a slightly improbable plaid jacket of Scotch tweed and in tight-fitting, royal blue breeches. Unfortunately this sartorial elegance is marred by his incredible facility for attracting vast quantities of filth to his person within minutes of the daily bath. Incidentally, he resents this unnatural intimacy with soap and water even more bitterly than does the average Tiblet and will only allow it on being heavily bribed in edible currency.

Life here would be hell if all Tiblets were Pooh-Bahs—but one little devil among hundreds of angels can have quite a pleasant leavening effect.

This afternoon Oliver and I went for a long hike through the forest, around the back of this mountain. We brought our bathing-togs as Doris had told us that a suitable swimming pool could be found if one kept walking long enough—and after about two hours we did reach the spot. Never have I bathed in such glorious surroundings. We were now at the head of a long, deep, narrowing valley, between high green mountains, where the splendour of this region's scenery reaches a superb climax. Here ends the precarious shepherd's path we had followed and the pool is suddenly visible, lying like an emerald between giant boulders. Above and below it the mountain torrent is fierce and foaming—a contrast which makes the tranquillity of the pool itself seem almost magical. Through the sparkling crystal of the water one sees its bed of silver sand, and in my haste to scramble down to this swimmer's paradise I very nearly broke an ankle on the wilderness of boulders. Oliver, I noticed, was a little less enthusiastic about immersion in Himalayan waters. However, he jumped in briskly and swam twenty yards to the other end of the pool—but there he jumped out even more briskly, roaring like a wounded lion. When he had thawed sufficiently to be able to articulate again he yelled frantically—'Dervla! Dervla! Come out of that wretched hell of water or you will begin to be not alive!' (In moments of stress he rather loses his linguistic grip.) I yelled back re-assuringly that I hadn't felt so alive for months—which was perfectly true, though I don't think I ever before swam in such icy water. Yet on emerging after about twenty minutes I felt not the slightest chill, despite the fact that the pool was now in shadow. Obviously this proves something, though I'm not sure what: possibly that the body stores heat and that after enduring horribly high temperatures for some months one is rewarded by developing an anti-chill device?

It's two months to-day since I came to the camp, yet because of weather and work this has been my first real exploration of its surroundings. Actually the region above and beyond Dall Lake is a lost little world of its own—high, still and very lovely, with the beauty of remote, unhurried places. One passes a couple of tiny farming hamlets, between Dall Lake and the pool, where the people are fair-skinned and aloof and tragically poor. The women's colourful costumes and massive jewellery reminded me of the nomads I met up the Kagan valley and the men, who wear home-spun clothes, usually have about twenty yards of cow-hair rope wound around their waists; most of them shepherd large flocks of sheep and goats on dangerous pastures at high altitudes. Around the hamlets these hill-folk cultivate the near vertical slopes with great skill, planting maize and potatoes on the narrow strips of laboriously irrigated terracing. (Incidentally, the potatoes here are as good as in Ireland, which is saying something!) Many of these families possess buffalo—beasts which I should have thought singularly unsuitable for such terrain—yet even a brief glimpse of the people and their dwellings shows that they live in virtually sub-human conditions of poverty, dirt and disease.

It's probably unavoidable that when working with refugees one becomes obsessed by their particular distress—but what a minor problem the Tibetans present in relation to the Colossus of misery that bestrides Asia! And in many ways refugees have an advantage over the rest since their homelessness and the political upheavals that make them refugees arouse sympathy and interest all over the world—whereas the pitiful Indian peasant is an unglamorous wretch representing a stale, dull problem in which public concern is not easily sustained. However, what one ordinary individual can do remains strictly limited, and by now, after my two months among the Tibetans, I know in my heart that I'm committed to them—much more for what they are giving me than vice versa. So it can profit me little to contemplate the vast arena of misery outside Tibland and—as Oliver would say—'It might become depressive' to think too much about it. Only people like Jill, with a genius for dedication in all directions at once, can effectively have a finger in every pie of need; yet perhaps it's wise to keep things in perspective by occasionally looking outside one's own little sphere of action.

8 OCTOBER

Since discovering the pool I've gone for a swim every Sunday and Tuesday (my day off) and last Sunday the excursion took a very zoological turn. To begin with I saw another—much bigger—troop of monkeys coming down from the heights. They flowed overhead like a grey river of fur, making odd twittering noises, and their passage from tree to tree created a lovely sound as of the whole forest swishing softly. Next, about half-a-mile further on, I saw my first Indian snake (apart from Delhi charmers' specimens). It was only about eighteen inches long and no thicker than your thumb, with very beautiful bright yellow markings on its nigger-brown skin. I'm told that 78% of the world's snakes are harmless and this was probably one of the majority but I didn't pick it up to find out.

Arriving at the pool, I disturbed a fascinating water-bird which I'd first observed up the Kagan valley. Somewhat larger than a thrush it has a jet-black back, snow-white top of head and cardinal red tail and breast—an enchanting sight as it flashes from the clear green water to the silver-grey rocks and back again. I was so intent on studying it that I had undressed and plunged into the pool before a movement from the top of a nearby rock caught my eye. Then I nearly drowned with excitement for there, lying in the sun about twenty-five feet above the water, was a magnificent leopard. His long tail and one big, soft cat-paw hung over the edge of the rock and his right ear was twitching backwards and forwards—but otherwise he showed no sign of being alarmed by my intrusion. This seemed very remarkable to me; however, Big Game Hunting is strictly prohibited in this area so perhaps he had no reason to think that the proximity of humans would interfere with his plans. Of course at that stage I didn't realize that he had plans, but later, when returning along the path, I could see that he was in fact closely observing a small herd of goats and kids grazing under the care of three children in a grassy depression on the far side of the river.

Leopards don't attack humans unless injured or cornered, or in defence of their young, but they cause havoc among the herds, and during the winter often kill village dogs. Apparently dog is one of their favourite foods and hapless live mongrels are used as baits when the locals want to trap and kill a particularly destructive marauder. Last week we heard that His Holiness had lost four of his tame deer to a leopard, and everyone in the camp was very upset about this, deer being especially precious animals to Tibetans because of their association with the Lord Buddha.

To-day my expedition to the pool provided excitement of another kind. When I left the camp after lunch the sun was hot and brilliant, but on the other side of the mountain, an hour later, big black clouds were visible, threatening the head of the valley. At first I thought nothing of this, assuming that it meant just one more brief thunderstorm such as we often have nowadays; yet I did notice that it got darker and darker as I went east up the valley, though behind me the sun was still shining with summer fervour from a blue sky. When I stopped half-way to survey the whole scene the lighting effects were tremendous—to the west the broad valley looked placid and innocent in golden light but to the east its narrowing depths were sullen and sinister beneath a mass of black cloud which had by now obscured the overhanging peaks.

As I reached the pool shattering thunder-crashes began to echo and re-echo between the mountain-walls, and soon after entering the water I was almost concussed by the most gigantic hail-stones I've ever seen—they were the size of ping-pong balls. I swam underwater to the shelter of a rock and then peered out hopefully, feeling that this sort of thing could not go on for long. Nor did it—a moment later the hail ceased, to be replaced by swirling snow. And that, as you might say, was the end of my swim. But the freakish thing is that the temperature didn't drop appreciably and I was quite warm walking home clad only in a shirt and shorts. Of course Oliver and Juliet were politely disbelieving when I reported my misadventure; the camp had enjoyed a flawlessly sunny afternoon, disturbed by no more than a few rumbles of distant thunder, and 'travellers' tales' of blizzards around the corner were just *too* incredible.

# 5

# *Some Queer Specimens*

We had terrific fun and games to-day. 'Meals for Millions' have decided to use us to test the value of their new protein food—an experiment which involves choosing 200 children, dividing them into six groups,and obtaining urine and stool specimens from each child.

First you take 200 little glass bottles and 200 little cardboard boxes and label them and write on each label a child's personal number, room number, age and sex. This is, shall we say, tedious—but at least you can get on with it. Next you sally forth to find your 200 Tiblets, present them with their containers and explain that now life is real, life is earnest and these so carefully labelled objects are not—repeat *not*—'gumchus', but are for the conservation of 'chimbathombhi' and 'chakathombhi'. The two- and three-year-olds regard such instructions as so much hot air and go off delightedly clutching their new toys and doubtless marvelling at the fact that Authority is actually *giving* them glass to play with.

In eighty-six cases we haven't yet found the children to match the waiting boxes and bottles. This is not altogether surprising, as in one room alone there are five 'Lobsangs'; unfortunately these are all boys, whereas the Lobsang we yearn for is a girl. Each child has at least two names (one given by its mother and one by the Lamas) and often a nickname as well for good measure, so by the time you've spent an hour looking for Pasang Thondup, only to find that he's really the child you've known for months as Sonam Dorje, your nerves are giving way. Nor are they restored by the discovery that about 25% of the personal numbers are now either lost or indecipherable. The whole experiment is farcical—what's the point of writing names and numbers on boxes and bottles when neither ayahs nor children can read? It's quite impossible for us personally to supervise the capturing of 400 specimens in the relevant containers; yet eventually these containers will be filled and solemnly handed over to the doctor in charge, who can only take the ayahs' word for it that their contents are according to specifications. Which just shows what reliance should be placed on the statistics so confidently announced after such experiments.

Last Saturday I was appalled to see a group of seven- and eight-year-olds poring over four American comics of the worst 'sex and violence' type. These degrading rags had been imported from Madras by one of the ayahs' sons—a fourteen-year-old who is at school there and has recently returned to the camp on vacation. With a splendid disregard for the Rights of the Individual I immediately confiscated the lot, gave their indignant owner a new Biro to fill the void and dumped the things in the kitchen stove. I can stand so much but I cannot stand American horror-comics being distributed among Tiblets. Granted my action was that of a crank; but for hours afterwards I was simmering with rage—not, obviously, against the Tiblets, but against the futility of my own gesture. These children really do have something worth preserving and the only name for it is innocence. It's difficult to enlarge on this without sounding like a minor Victorian poetess, but compared to the Tiblets our children, with their sophistication and precocity, are terrifying indications of the depths to which Western civilization has sunk.

The other day I chanced on an interesting discovery. A father had come to visit his daughters and around his neck hung two handsome silver medallions—each about the size of a half-crown—which at once attracted my attention. I asked if I might examine them more closely and was considerably astonished to find that they were very old Catholic medals, inscribed in Latin. The inscriptions were no longer entirely legible, yet their Catholicity was beyond doubt. My enquiries as to their origin led nowhere; the owner only knew that these were powerful religious charms which had been in his family for many generations. His home village lies between Lhasa and Sikkim so the medals may well be mementoes of the seventeenth century French Jesuits who visited Lhasa.

This man was one of those parents who occasionally come to take their children away for a holiday with the family. He disappeared down the track to Forsythe Bazaar looking very happy, with four-year-old Pasang riding on his back and six-year-old Thondup grasping his hand firmly while chattering away nineteen to the dozen. In about a month's time they will return from the Kulu valley, accompanied by their young brother Norbu, who has just been weaned.

Some Westerners strongly disapprove of these vacations, arguing that it is unwise for the children to return to their squalid parental tents. But health is not an exclusively physical thing, and unless a child is seriously ill it's difficult to believe that reunion with an affectionate family can do anything but good.

Recently we have had a few tricky cases, when parents wished to remove very sick children who were receiving treatment in the Dispensary. The parents did not realize that taking their offspring to a road-camp could have fatal consequences and they remained unconvinced by Oliver's arguments. This brought us up against the problem of a Parent's Right to Decide but in the end we threw such abstract speculations overboard and simply refused to allow the children to leave. I'm by no means sure that this is the correct thing to do; yet in such a situation one tends to assume that superior scientific knowledge automatically confers the right to defy parental wishes—just as on Saturday I took it upon myself to censor the Tiblets' reading matter. The consequences, when dealing with adults, are rather distressing, involving an unavoidable degree of bullying and the treating of the insistent, anxious parents as though they were inferior beings. Fortunately in all these cases the children recovered, which they most probably would not have done had they been moved. However, even this does not satisfy me that our action was justified. Perhaps in the West we lay a little too much emphasis on the preservation of life at all costs and we never can understand why everyone else doesn't share our demonstrably 'sensible' views on such subjects. But other people have other standards and who are we forcibly to replace them merely because they contravene our sense of right and wrong?

18 OCTOBER

The 'Meals for Millions' fun and games continued to-day. All bottles and boxes had to be delivered at the Dispensary by seven o'clock this morning, and at nine o'clock the doctor, with his team of laboratory technicians, came sweating up the hill. An hour later I heard a roar of rage from the mobile laboratory and the doctor came striding towards me, furiously brandishing a test-tube and almost foaming at the mouth. His anger made for incoherence, but I soon gathered that in a bottle supposedly containing the urine of a two-year-old boy he had found the urine of a pregnant ayah. He was not soothed when I collapsed with laughter and showed no sign of surprise or resentment— after working among Tibetans for two and a half months one knows exactly what degree of co-operation to expect from them in conducting a scientific investigation. And personally if I were an ayah in charge of fifty or sixty children and were given thirty or forty bottles and boxes, neatly labelled in a language I couldn't read, with instructions to have the right specimens in the right containers at the right time, I, too, would do exactly what the harassed ayah did. There's a place for everything and Dharamsala Camp is not the place for large-scale experiments.

We've had quite a number of visitors here since the monsoon ended. David Williams from Kasauli has been three times, in connection with the building of the new dispensary, and Stuart Menteth has twice come from Simla on S.C.F. business. Various other characters also drift in and out, since His Holiness's presence in the area has turned Dharamsala into a place of pilgrimage or a tourist attraction—depending on the visitor's outlook. One young Englishman named Mike stayed with us for three weeks and was a tremendous help; being a practical type he worked like a navvy, yet still had time to form a most successful Mutual Admiration Society with the Tiblets. But some visitors are merely a nuisance, as they float around making obvious remarks and impeding the routine. And worst of all are the Febs and Fabs (Female European Buddhists and Female American Buddhists) who flock here to have an audience—or if possible audiences—with His Holiness, and who are apt to come all over Theosophist without warning and to stare fixedly at you asking rude questions about your soul. It's a sad fact (doubtless of profound psychosomatic significance) that when anyone starts talking to me about my soul I am sorely tempted to giggle: a reaction which Theosophists cannot but regard as impolite, or blasphemous—or both. I don't for one moment doubt these women's sincerity, but my opinion on the matter was very precisely expressed by Carl Jung when he wrote: 'I have serious doubts as to the blessings of Western civilization, and I have similar misgivings as to the adoption of Eastern spirituality by the West.' Febs and Fabs makes me feel as uncomfortable as do Indian Christians—in both cases one is aware of something artificial somewhere, of a strange unease and of a vocal self-consciousness about aspects of life that most of us can at least appear to take in our stride, though we may have inward conflicts about them. But the involuntary hostility aroused by those who adopt alien philosophies is probably mainly due to a basic suspicion that they are guilty of attempting to escape from their inherited responsibilities. It may be argued that the majority of Westerners are no longer true to the traditions of Christendom, and are perhaps all the worse off for this, but instead of leaving the sinking ship they do at least make what they regard as the necessary modification's within the traditional framework of their own civilization.

23 OCTOBER

At last it's getting really cold after sunset and now I sit wrapped in a blanket when writing. This morning Juliet decided that we would have to abandon the daily bathing; under present weather conditions it becomes a straight choice between pneumonia and scabies. We all regret this bitterly, as great things were being achieved; when one compares the scabies situation three months ago and now, the improvement is almost unbelievable. In an effort to keep the mite under control, despite the cold weather, Oliver has had mud ranges built in the open, both here and outside the Dispensary, and on these the children's clothes will be boiled regularly—a reversal of monsoon conditions, when the bodies could be washed but the clothes couldn't!

Other heartening improvements have also taken place, including some alleviation of the overcrowding problem through the reduction of the total camp numbers to about 700; the other hundreds have been transferred to Mussoorie or Dalhousie. Most mportant of all, sufficient pressure has been brought to bear in the relevant quarters, and from now on every child in the camp is to receive one piece of fresh fruit per diem—at the moment a banana, later in the season an orange.

The first day's distribution of fruit ended in chaos because of the aforementioned Tibetan tendency to hoard food. That night we found scores of peeled, half-eaten bananas concealed in the children's 'pouches'—and it's difficult to think of anything less suitable than a peeled banana for storage next to the skin *outside* the stomach. So next day Juliet got things organized and now, at 3 p.m., it's the accepted routine for all the children to line up on the compound, receive their banana, peel it and *eat* it in its entirety before the ranks may be broken. As yet the Tiblets haven't learned not to drop the peels on the ground, and the sweepers have an extra job each day. But Juliet plans to combine a lesson in civic spirit with the absorption of vitamins and by to-morrow litter-boxes will be installed and their purpose explained so, knowing Tiblets, I'm sure a banana-skin will never again be seen on the compound.

To-day was cloudy and, once the sun had disappeared, just about as cold as late October in Ireland. This was disappointing as it's a day of celebration in the camp—the forty-ninth day after Rinchin's death and so the end of her 'Bardo' life and the beginning of a new life in another incarnation. I've just paused to check on the calendar, which tells me that in fact it's only forty-three days since the death—a typical Tibetan calculation! The little hut on the mountain-side was reopened this morning (Dubkay now lives elsewhere—or nowhere) and again became a shrine where all day three Lamas sat chanting prayers opposite the effigy, while hundreds of butter-lamps flickered beneath a picture of the Lord Buddha, and outside, on a level, grassy ledge, a mud-stove was built to cook the celebration banquet. The entire kitchen staff migrated up for the day and here our lunch and dinner were prepared, since on this occasion Dubkay was host to everyone in the camp. I can't imagine what most of the dishes were, but each tasted more delicious than the last and one felt quite immobilized after the final course. The children were given 'tormas' and released from school this morning and all the adults spent the day sitting in rows near the stove, either preparing or eating food while drinking immeasurable quantities of 'chang'. To my great sorrow no one offered us any of this—perhaps it isn't considered fit for Western consumption. But at least one Westerner would have been very glad to consume a pint of it. . . .

Yesterday the Indian radio broadcast a report that a widespread revolt against the Chinese is imminent in Tibet and to-day the Tibetans here are discussing the possibility of Russia moving in to 'help' their country should any organized uprising take place. Recently All-India Radio also announced that since China annexed Tibet the death-rate there had risen by 50% as the Lamas, with their herbal medicines and charms, had been replaced by quack Chinese doctors. This statement amused us intensely. Disregarding any comparisons between modern and Tibetan medicine, how does anyone know what the death-rate in Tibet was before 1950? Listening to the solemn voice of the announcer one would think that Tibet had held a national census every five years—how unrealistic can propaganda get!

To-night we heard the President's United Nations' Day speech to the nation—a truly inspiring effort, free of the usual platitudes. I've always known of Dr Radhakrishnan as a most remarkable man, though I've never read anything of his, and this speech revealed a most delightful personality as well as a brilliant brain.

### 27 October

Now autumn has really come, though not in our blazing way. Going for my swim this afternoon I noticed that many mosses and ferns have turned to golden brown, a few yellowed leaves are being shed and a magnificent crimson creeper is flowing through the branches from tree to tree. Himalayan orchids—the only one of the variegated wild flowers that I can recognize—are still flowering, but otherwise there is the familiar sense of nature relaxing and growth ceasing. There are more of the small snakes, of which I had seen only one before, and birds are also more numerous. Superb eagles are following the flocks down from the heights, and this afternoon two of them were visible below me as I walked along the high path to the pool. They went sailing easily along the course of the river, all grace and effortless power. The goat, sheep, kid and lamb traffic was dense on this hitherto deserted path, and once I had to wait, before crossing an insecure moraine, to allow hundreds of the creatures to pass first. When I reached the pool and plunged in the water was so icy that for a few moments I couldn't breathe: yet on emerging after about ten minutes I found the air-temperature adequately warm and even to-day my hands didn't turn blue, as they so often do at home after swimming in water far less cold than this.

Early yesterday morning Oliver and I took a meningitis case down to the Civil Hospital in Lower Dharamsala. For such purposes the camp has the use of a station-wagon, presented to His Holiness by one of the Canadian charities, and as we were being driven slowly down the winding road we saw three young hill-men walking through the trees. One of them had his head roughly swathed in a blood-soaked bandage and was being half carried by the others, so we stopped to take them on. The injured man sat in the front, his companions got in behind, and as we continued towards the hospital we achieved a complicated feat of multi-translation. One of the hill-men told our Tibetan driver, who speaks Hindi but no English, what had happened. Then the driver told a fellow-Tibetan, who speaks a little English but no Hindi, and finally, through him, Oliver and I heard the sad story.

At dusk on the previous evening the injured man had been attacked by a bear while collecting firewood at the edge of the forest some quarter of a mile from the camp. After being violently knocked down he at once picked himself up and attempted to run away—but this further enraged the bear, which promptly levelled him again, severely mauling his face, neck and head. (Seemingly bears always go for the jugular vein.) Luckily the poor chap lost consciousness at this stage and the bear, presuming him dead, made off. Soon after he came to and dragged himself home, where his wife bathed and bandaged the appalling gashes. But it was then too late to begin the long walk to the hospital, so the patient spent a night of agony before setting out at dawn with his friends' assistance. One is repeatedly astounded by the powers of endurance of these frail-looking peasants. To-day we heard that the patient is making good progress, though without plastic surgery he will remain dreadfully disfigured for life.

For the past week a European family—father, mother and three children—has been living in the Dak-bugalow in Lower Dharamsala and visiting the camp daily. One of their children is Lhamo, a Tibetan girl who was 'adopted by post' and sent from Dharamsala to their home in the South of India three years ago. She is now aged five and their own children are aged six and four. Curiously enough Lhamo is the first sulky, unfriendly Tiblet I've ever met, though the family background to which she was transferred couldn't be better—a happy young couple, deeply interested in and sympathetic towards Tibet in a remarkably balanced way, children who are genuinely fond of their adopted sister and a Tibetan ayah, strict but kind, who is supposed to keep Lhamo in touch with her own religion, language and culture. Everything here favours successful integration in a Western family, yet so far the experiment seems to be a failure and the parents are now considering the adoption of another Tiblet (our Sonam Nobo?) to see if this might help sort Lhamo out. The family plan to stay here for three weeks to give the child a chance to *feel* Tibetan, but obviously the whole thing is a devastating muddle from her point of view. However, some slight advances have been made this past week, during which she has spent all day with the other Tiblets. One of Lhamo's 'things' concerns language; at home she stubbornly refuses to speak Tibetan though her ayah has ensured that she can understand it. But here, when the family firmly abandon her on the compound each morning, she must speak her own language if she wishes to utter again before evening; and I notice that she is gaining in fluency each day, as she prays, eats and plays with the rest. (Her mother shows a rare lack of fussiness in permitting her to partake of camp food: very few Westerners would encourage this degree of re-integration.) In other respects too—less self-importance and more laughter—this policy of amalgamation is paying dividends. Incidentally, it's interesting to observe how unquestioningly the other Tiblets have accepted the return to the fold of a comrade who has so obviously attained a privileged position from the material point of view.

Namgyal and his son

Procession of High Lamas arriving at the nursery

Incarnate Lamas
blessing the
babies

A family of
Indian hill-
farmers near
the camp

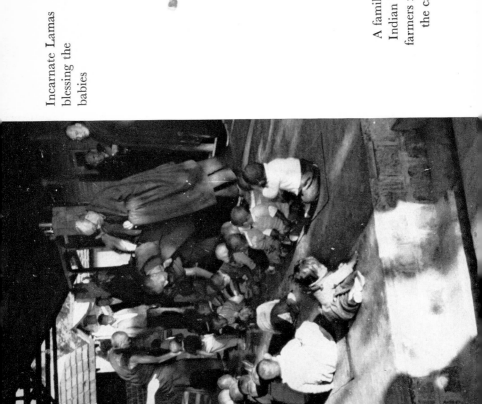

# 6

## *The Dalai Lama*

Before breakfast to-day a message came from the Palace summoning me to that formal audience which His Holiness grants to all those who work with Tibetans. Inevitably, I spent the rest of the morning looking forward to meeting the man who represents that aspect of Tibetan life which most attracts, repels or bewilders foreigners.

The majority of Tibetans do not themselves understand why the Dalai Lama means what he does to them, yet their feeling for him is their strongest corporate emotion; he is more revered than was ever the greatest saint in Christendom and more loved and deferred to than the greatest king. This relationship between the man and his people, which has little to do with the personality of the individual Dalai Lama, is a singular development of certain Mahayana Buddhist beliefs and Tibetans never think of His Holiness as a mere man.

It is an absurd over-simplification to refer to the Dalai Lama as Tibet's 'god-king' and the popularity of this term reveals our necessarily limited understanding of Eastern philosophy. Within Tibet itself the equally limited understanding of the peasants has had much the same effect; by them His Holiness is regarded as being, personally, a god in the simplest sense of the word. But few things are simple in Buddhism, and the educated Tibetan interprets his ruler's position very differently, regarding him as a vessel which contains the Spirit of Chenrezig, a being who out of compassion for all living things has waived his right to Nirvana and remains on earth, through repeated incarnations, to help the less fortunate attain a spiritual state which will make them also worthy of Nirvana.

It would be very pleasant if one could accept this straightforward and touching account of the Dalai Lama's function and

H

forget the endless political intrigues which simmered, bubbled, and occasionally boiled over as a result of the unique method of choosing a new Dalai Lama. Before the Communist invasion Tibet was a peaceful country where an exceptionally likeable people lived frugally yet contentedly: but the facts compel us to admit that this was despite, rather than because of, the peculiar status of its ruler.

In 1640 Ngawang Lobsang Gyatso became the first Dalai Lama to assume both spiritual and temporal power over the whole of Tibet. During his lifetime the building of the Potala was begun, and one of his government ministers, Senge Gyatso, concealed his death for some years in order to complete the building of the Palace, and then chose his successor. This choice proved unfortunate, since the sixth Dalai Lama was the Tibetan Borgia: in between love affairs he wrote what is almost the only romantic poetry in the language, instead of applying himself to a study of the scriptures. After he had been slain by the Mongols no effective ruler succeeded until the late nineteenth century. Then Thupten Gyatso, the Thirteenth Dalai Lama, reached his majority and this great man reigned wisely until 1933, restoring his country's *de facto* independence.

Only the most pig-headed idealist could ignore the consequences of the Tibetan system of seeking out a child, bringing him to the Potala and having him grow up there under the exclusive guidance of a Regency Council who may justly, if not reverently, be referred to as the ruling clique. Human nature is human nature, even in Tibet, and the political opportunities offered by such a system were frequently found irresistible; this is proved by the mysterious deaths—between 1805 and 1874—of four young Dalai Lamas as they were about to assume power.

Even when the Dalai Lama survives this dangerous stage the extent of his actual power remains questionable since so much depends on the calibre of his mentors and on their training of the young man who, at eighteen, becomes—at least theoretically—such a power in the land.

If he sincerely believes in himself as the vehicle of the Spirit of Chenrezig it is beyond our imagination to grasp the effect of this belief on a Dalai Lama's mind and emotions. But if he does not entirely believe in himself the suspicion that he is being used to perpetrate a colossal hoax must have a profoundly horrible influence. It is unlikely, however, that many Dalai Lamas have doubted their function; to argue otherwise is to imply that one of the world's greatest religions is no more than a cynical conspiracy. As they grew to maturity these men were securely surrounded by the customs and rituals of a purely Lamaist environment and, though we tend to confuse the ignoring with the rejecting of religious principles, it is obvious that genuine faith co-existed with corruption and power-grabbing in the court—as it did in the Renaissance Papal Courts. However, one doubts if any Dalai Lama, suddenly confronted by the sceptical, analytical twentieth century, could retain his conventional faith in his own status. Essentially he might well remain a truly devout Buddhist, but he is bound to experience considerable conflict on the issue of his personal position. And this, it seems, is exactly what has happened to the Fourteenth Dalai Lama.

Recently His Holiness helped to draft the new Tibetan Constitution with its revolutionary clause naming him as 'The Chief Executive of the Government and the Religious Leader of the Tibetan People . . . subject to the deprivation of his powers in the highest interest of the State'. This clause can only be interpreted to mean that the Tibetans must no longer look upon the Dalai Lama as an incarnation of Chenrezig, since no human authority could deprive a Bodhisattva of his powers. Among the ordinary refugees the promulgation of the Constitution caused horror and grief and it was repudiated by them as being totally unacceptable. Then the tragic irony of the whole situation became apparent, for the Constitution also guarantees democracy based on the tenets of Buddhism—and the first result of 'democracy', if it were in fact operating among the Tibetans, would be a vigorous denial of the State's right to interfere with the absolute power of the Dalai Lama. As Miss Loïs Lang-Sims has written: '. . . this is but one aspect of the total *impasse* in which the Tibetan community now finds itself.'

At 2 p.m. His Holiness's car arrived to bring me to the Palace —a courtesy term used to describe the big British-built bungalow where the Tibetan ruler has lived since 1960. A strong guard of the Punjab Armed Police is on duty here night and day, patrolling the grounds and environs and checking the credentials of every visitor. It was 2.25 by the time my passport had been dealt with, innumerable forms filled in, a phone call made to the Palace to ensure that someone of my name really was expected and the various sentries satisfied. Then, punctually at 2.30, Mr Sonam—His Holiness's chief interpreter—conducted me into the presence of the Dalai Lama.

Where someone of His Holiness's stature is concerned there are probably as many different versions of the man as there are people who meet him; unavoidably one has one's instinctive personal reactions. One also has certain preconceptions and it would be untrue to say that I met the Dalai Lama with an open mind; all my conversations with those who knew him had led me to expect an outstanding individual—not necessarily likeable, but certainly a Personality. Instead I found myself talking to a simple, pleasant young man, who has the gracious manner and lively humour of the average Tibetan but who failed to impress me by any unusual qualities—apart from a total lack of egotism, which by our standards is remarkable enough in the circumstances.

On meeting some High Lamas one spontaneously recognizes them as deeply religious men, yet with the Dalai Lama I had no awareness of being in the presence of an ascetic whose life is centred on things spiritual. This is not to imply that His Holiness's life is otherwise centred; it may merely be that he is as yet too immature to convey such a feeling to others.

However, half an hour's conversation convinced me that here was a ruler whose chief concern would always be the welfare of his people—though unfortunately he showed no sign of an intellectual ability equal to the enormous task of solving their present problems. But I was also becoming increasingly aware of a certain tension in the atmosphere. I felt that the Dalai Lama was constantly on his guard, that he was unsure of himself in dealing with foreigners and that he was continually attempting to gauge my reactions to him. One can only pity the vulnerability of this sensitive young man, who is so often exposed to the relentless scrutiny of a world either politely sceptical or impatiently contemptuous of the values which he represents.

I NOVEMBER

The weather to-day made me feel quite homesick. This morning the sky was overcast and dark, with a late autumn stillness and a chilliness in the air. Then, after lunch, the rain started and it's been a brute of a day ever since—icy gale winds are blowing sheets of sleet across the compound at the moment. Obviously these conditions greatly increase the sufferings of undernourished children, and it's heartbreaking to see the Tiblets all purple and shivering as they snuggle up to you for warmth. They still go barefooted and are wearing the same wretched scraps of clothing given them during the summer. Their bedding too is hopelessly inadequate, despite the announcement recently made by Mr Jamieson (Director of Operations at the U.N. High Commission for Refugees at Geneva) that if all the relief supplies sent to India had been distributed there should now be one and a half blankets available for every Tibetan refugee.

We're going to have an interesting, but I should think exhausting, weekend, as a staggering number of visitors are expected to-morrow; viz. the Menteths from Simla, with Jenny Westropp, an English S.C.F. nurse who also works there; Mr and Mrs Burke, S.C.F. representatives from Canada; Sigrid Arnd, representing the Swiss Tibetan Homesteads; Mrs Freda Bedi, who runs the Young Lama School at Dalhousie; Mr Peters, head of the Indian Y.M.C.A. and M. and Mme Neufe, from Switzerland. M. Neufe is head of the Y.M.C.A. World Organization for Refugees and is therefore the chief V.I.P. of the lot, as the Y.M.C.A. has, to date, done more than anyone else for this camp. That makes a total of ten V.I.P.s and the odd thing is that their simultaneous arrival here is a coincidence. However, from the camp authorities' point of view it's a convenient coincidence; those 'improvements' in the children's conditions which are habitually faked to impress V.I.P.s need not now be repeated too often. The present hustle to smarten things up all over the camp would be amusing if it were not enraging. It's a pity that V.I.P.s are too 'I' to arrive unannounced and see for themselves the true state of things, before going home to write their reports.

2 NOVEMBER

Mrs Tsiring Dolma is becoming more and more difficult to deal with. Last week I had a flaming row with her when she most unjustly attacked Doris and Jill in my presence, and to-day it was S.C.F.'s turn to struggle with her incomprehensible attitudes.

The Menteths and Jenny are to take nine of our most delicate children to fill vacant places at Stirling Castle, and it so happens that among these is a very weakly eight-year-old orphan boy, nicknamed 'the doctor's friend'. (He and Oliver are as attached as Cama Yishy and I.) One of the camp rules is that no orphan may be transferred elsewhere and one of S.C.F.'s rules is that no child over the age of five may be admitted to their Simla Homes; but naturally when Oliver explained that Tsiring Thondup's chances of survival would be increased by a removal to Simla the Menteths agreed to make an exception to their rule and the next step was to obtain a similar concession from Mrs Tsiring Dolma. Then the fun started. The Menteths, Juliet, Jenny, Oliver, Mrs Tsiring Dolma, Mr Phalla, an interpreter and myself sat together in our little room for over an hour having what began as a discussion and ended as a verbal free fight. Mrs Tsiring Dolma made outrageous accusations against S.C.F. but the Menteths showed superhuman restraint by not losing their tempers and doggedly attempted to keep the conversation on a reasonable level for Tsiring Thondup's sake. One could hardly describe us as 'arguing' since there was really no basis for argument; Mrs Tsiring Dolma simply repeated at regular intervals 'There is a rule that no orphan can leave the camp and we cannot break our own rules.' I asked three times whether the rules or the children were of prime importance but that tiresome question was ignored. In the end Mrs Tsiring Dolma won the unfair contest; she has absolute control over the children here and the issue had never really been in doubt. When she left poor Oliver was nearly in tears, Stuart was swearing like a trooper, Pauline looked exhausted and for the first time I saw Juliet's composure show signs of cracking.

The most obvious explanation of this incident is also the most uncharitable one, but knowing Mrs Tsiring Dolma as we now do it must be considered as a possibility. Undoubtedly she has compensated herself for the loss of the nation-wide power she enjoyed in Tibet by asserting her authority here beyond all reasonable limits and as she clearly resents higher standards of living being provided for Tiblets elsewhere our argument to-day that Tsiring Thondup would be more likely to survive in Simla must have infuriated her.

This whole incident illustrates some of the typical hazards met with in the world of Tibetan officialdom. One can't help feeling on occasions that there must be powerful motives, of which we are completely ignorant, behind certain baffling and apparently stupid Tibetan attitudes. Actually we know too little about these people even to begin to understand why they act and speak as they do. In the present case there could be alternative (or complementary) reasons to the one already suggested as an explanation of Mrs Tsiring Dolma's unco-operativeness. For instance, Tsiring Thondup may be an Incarnate Lama (it's strongly rumoured that some of our children are) or there could be other grounds, more convincing than his orphan state but unimaginable to us, why he should not be moved to Simla. But the Tibetans, maintaining their traditional xenophobic policy, are always reluctant to clarify these situations. This is especially regrettable when so many of us are anxious to be given the opportunity to understand and would be willing, where possible, to adjust our demands to their outlook.

Another hazard, highlighted during this afternoon's performance, is the problem of communication. The Palace interpreters are just as fluent as native English speakers, but one often senses that they are being slightly selective in their translations —particularly if home-truths are emanating from one or both sides. Personally I don't blame them for this; if I were constantly in Mrs Tsiring Dolma's company I'd be very careful indeed not to translate anything that might worsen her temper during the next twenty-four hours. And if they tone down some of her remarks I'm sure their motives are the best; they must be even more conscious than we are of her 'difficultness' and, being intelligent, kind-hearted girls, they obviously don't wish to see bad being made worse. However, none of this helps us to cope with the complexities of communication, which reflect not only the vast difference between two languages, but between two modes of thought and standards of behaviour. Because national characteristics influence language there is room for misunderstanding—often absurd and occasionally tragic—even in conversation with Tibetans who speak English or German fluently.

This morning the weather paid its best respects to our invasion of V.I.P.s and we enjoyed a crisp, sunny day after the storm. I noticed that one of the 'improvements' for the visitors' benefit consists in the removal from their posts of our juvenile sentries. One evening, about a month ago, I registered the fact that for the past few days pairs of the older Tiblets had been sitting continuously at each of the three paths leading into the Lower Nursery—and the odd thing was that even at meal-times they remained 'in situ' and had their food brought to them. My enquiries about this curious phenomenon were met with embarrassed evasions: but of course we soon learned that Mrs Tsiring Dolma had instituted a system whereby throughout the entire nursery pairs of children were on guard at each approach during all the daylight hours, so that she might receive immediate warning if anyone entered the camp without her permission. Even when the bad weather came the unfortunate children remained—characteristically—true to their post and to-day was the first occasion on which the watch was relaxed.

## 10 NOVEMBER

To-day Lhamo and her adoptive family left Dharamsala—in a sadly frustrated condition. Last week they decided, after considerable thought, to attempt to adopt Sonam Nobo (now renamed Tenzing Chockla by the Lamas)—not simply to provide Lhamo with a little Tibetan brother but also because they had, after a fortnight's acquaintance, fallen hopelessly in love with the infant. Their intention was to care for and educate him, without separating him from Dubkay, whom they were also willing to 'adopt' and train as their chauffeur-cum-gardener. Everyone was agreed that for the sakes of all concerned this would be an excellent plan, and Dubkay, who has always been obsessively interested in cars, was thrilled to think that soon he might be learning how to drive and maintain one of these magic chariots.

However, in this set-up it's one thing to seek permission for such a scheme and another thing to get it. Lhamo's family are soon returning to Europe and 'there is a rule' that for the future no more Tiblets may be adopted by Western families. So that was that.

When the scheme was first discussed and I heard Dubkay approve, but say that the decision was Mrs Tsiring Dolma's rather than his, my Western hackles rose instantly. Here was a man of thirty-one (my own age!) being offered a never-to-be-repeated chance of advancement for himself and his son, yet not being free to accept it. In spite of personal misgivings about dispersing the Tibetan community and settling children in the West my immediate reaction was a standard European upsurge of fury and indignation; everything that matters most to us is outraged by such a curtailment of liberty.

It is very difficult to think objectively on a subject like this, but we must beware of using the wrong yardstick. When Mrs Tsiring Dolma's decision was announced our bloods boiled in unison, yet Dubkay appeared to be completely unperturbed. Yes, he would have liked to take advantage of this generous offer—but only if those in authority approved. He is not a subtle or reserved man and if he had felt any resentment at being thwarted I doubt if he could have concealed it and simulated that cheerful unconcern with which he greeted the verdict. To us such an incident is symptomatic of a monstrous serfdom, to Dubkay it is merely an occasion for showing a natural dependence on the superior wisdom of one's rulers. And though we would not consider the bargain a good one he has, in exchange for his personal liberty, a carefree existence on which no problems intrude because what might create them is always someone else's responsibility. Also, in fairness to the Tibetan Government, we should remember that similar restrictions limit the freedom of movement of Indian nationals, though theoretically India is a fully-fledged modern democracy.

The wisdom of the decision made in this case is obviously debatable. On the one hand Lhamo's adoption has not been very successful so far and the same goes for other Tiblets adopted by Western families. Therefore, since the preservation of Tibetan culture can be best served by keeping the refugees united

and since Dubkay is already congenially—if not very construc-
tively—employed among his own people, it seems that the
decision is justified.

On the other hand this could be considered as one of those
exceptional cases where general principles are not the best
guide. The family concerned are themselves exceptional in the
extent of their understanding sympathy for the Tibetans. They
would certainly encourage Sonam Nobo eventually to return to
his own people as a doctor or teacher—and in this Dubkay,
from what I know of him, would fully support them. Admittedly
such a plan is always experimental, and for its success depends
almost entirely on the character of the child. But it could be
argued that the gamble is worth while when the prize might be
another trained Tibetan to work among the next generation of
refugees, wherever they may then be settled.

Yesterday evening Lhamo's family invited us all down to a
farewell dinner in the Dak-bungalow. This was a rather sad
occasion, for during their three weeks here these people became
very much part of the camp, and their kindness and gaiety
considerably brightened our lives. After dinner we went to the
local cinema where I saw my first—and I sincerely hope my
last—Hindi film. It was supposed to be superb, one of the best
ever, but to me it seemed too boring for description. And it
lasted for hours. Oliver very sensibly went to sleep after fifteen
minutes, was wakened at the interval and returned to sleep
immediately on resumption of play. Juliet, who likes everything
Indian, enjoyed it thoroughly; I planned a new article and our
host and hostess hunted fleas, of which there were an inordinate
number in the immediate vicinity. By the time we were released
at 11 p.m. it had become bitterly cold and the sky was ablaze
with a frosty glitter of stars.

A few days ago we had another unpleasant altercation with
Mrs Tsiring Dolma. This time Oliver was chiefly involved: it
seems criminally preposterous that a doctor's advice should be
ignored unless it happens to coincide with the personal whims
of a lay-person.

On the morning of the 7th Oliver said that Dowa, one of the
cobblers from the Upper Nursery, must go to Ludhiana Hospital for immediate cancer tests—but of course the poor man

couldn't leave the camp without Mrs Tsiring Dolma's permission, and this was refused. Oliver then wrote to her at the Palace, pointing out the extreme urgency of the case, but a verbal reply came back saying, 'This man may not leave the camp on any account!' No reason for refusing permission was even hinted at this time and we quite missed the familiar phrase 'there is a rule . . .' But here again one surmises some strong unknown motive operating beneath the surface—though when we are so consistently excluded from 'what goes on' it becomes increasingly difficult to make allowances of this sort. However, political factors could be concerned here; rumours are frequent about the presence of Communist sympathizers among the adults in this camp and if Dowa was a suspect neither the Tibetan nor Indian authorities would wish to have him at liberty in Ludhiana. (The Indians are understandably very alert to the dangers of Chinese spies masquerading as Tibetan refugees; quite a few cases have already been proved, and in consequence the movements of Tibetans in India are closely watched.)

On receiving this verbal reply to his letter Oliver's next step was to seek a personal interview with Mrs Tsiring Dolma: but this only made the whole thing look more sinister. Dowa himself was at the interview and was made to say (or the interpreter was made to say that he had said . . .) that he didn't wish to leave the camp and knew he was free to go if he wanted to. At this stage in a Tibetan intrigue I usually find myself being disarmed by the sheer naïvety of the manœuvres. Only a very unsophisticated opponent could hope to deceive us by such a move, for on the previous day Dowa's eagerness to go to hospital had been quite pathetic.

After this *débâcle* Oliver returned to the Dispensary in an understandably filthy temper and announced that he was going to write another, more vehement letter on the subject—in fact he declared that he would make it 'a rude and strong letter'. But this is easier said than done for someone like Oliver; he is temperamentally incapable of being rude, whatever the provocation, and the letter which he showed me after supper was firm but polite. I hinted that his courtly polish might perhaps be wasted on the recipient and poor Oliver looked very worried and said, 'You think it is not rude enough?' 'No,' I replied, 'it's not nearly rude enough—but if I may make a few emendations . . .?' To this Oliver somewhat nervously agreed and I saw him flinch when the 'emendations' were completed. But for Dowa's sake he put his gallantry aside and retyped and signed the letter. Thupten, his bearer, then delivered it to the Palace and at 5.30 a.m. on the following morning Dowa left for Ludhiana.

# 7

# Politics and Parents

12 NOVEMBER

Within the past few weeks I've been analysing more closely the part this camp plays in the Tibetan refugee tragedy and my conclusions have made me a little uneasy about the gay abandon with which agencies devote money to the project. One wonders if they are aware of the exact nature of the operation they have chosen to subsidize.

On my arrival in July, I took the situation at its face-value; Dharamsala Nursery was a refuge for children whose parents were unable to care for them and who would probably die of neglect if they couldn't come here. Undoubtedly this is partly true. Some of these children could not survive outside a camp, and it must be admitted that when the Nursery was opened in 1960 the need for such a centre was urgent. But now things are changing; parents are obtaining employment and finding their bearings—yet more and more children have been coming to a camp where, until very recently, 'conditions were worse than in any European refugee camp immediately after World War II', to quote the comment of an experienced observer. After living here for some time a strange element in the atmosphere seeps into one's consciousness and gradually one begins to suspect that philanthropy is not the sole *raison d'être* of the Dharamsala Tibetan Refugee Nursery.

My doubts on this matter first crystallized about a month ago, when I observed how strongly Mrs Tsiring Dolma resented influential visitors being told that the numbers of children were lessening slightly—an item of news which we passed on joyfully as an indication of some improvement in the general situation. However, the Nursery Principal was very quick to intervene in these conversations and to impress on visitors the fact that soon our numbers would be higher than ever and that more and more funds would be needed to maintain the camp. This 'prophecy' has in fact been fulfilled during the past week; many of the hundreds of Tibetans who recently came here from the road-camps on a pilgrimage have now left their children at the Nursery.

The motives behind these parental decisions are disturbing. Soon after Mrs Tsiring Dolma's show of displeasure at the reduction in our numbers a very reliable source informed me that Lamas are regularly despatched from Dharamsala to the road-camps with instructions to encourage parents to bring their children here—and at this stage I began to smell a large and unpleasant rat. I then decided to collect a few statistics, with the aid of a dependable interpreter. To date I've questioned seventy-three parents, asking them why they brought their children here, what they wished their children to do when they leave and what their own financial position is at the moment. In 100% of cases the reply to the first question was that they brought the children here to be educated—and the majority added that they also wished them to be near His Holiness. In reply to the second question seventy-one out of seventy-three said that when their children leave here they would like them to do 'whatever His Holiness wishes'; the remaining two very boldly stated that they wanted their sons to go to Switzerland and become Western-style doctors. (It is interesting that both these fathers were themselves 'am-chis' in Tibet.) In reply to the third question fifty-six out of the seventy-three said that they were earning coolie wages on the road-camps; the other seventeen certainly could not have supported their children, being in poor health and dependent on begging or on the generosity of relatives.

These figures give so much food for thought that after considering them over a period of days one begins to suffer from cerebral indigestion. To me it is profoundly shocking that 100% of parents gave 'educational opportunities' as the chief reason for bringing their children to this camp. It isn't natural for Tibetan peasants to think in such terms, except concerning those children who are destined to be monks—and even then it is not the educational advantage of a monastic career that weighs most with the average Tibetan peasant. Therefore this rotten carrot of 'schooling' must have been deliberately dangled as part of the campaign to keep Dharamsala camp crammed. And it's a *very* rotten carrot because, as I've already made clear, the 'education' available in the Lower Nursery is farcical even by Indian standards. What really infuriates me is the apparent meanness of this deception—it's intolerable to think of these docile, trusting peasants, who are so bewildered by our complicated world, being unscrupulously exploited for the benefit of the very people from whom they seek guidance. Even if one allowed that some parents are capable of calculating that their children have a chance of being transferred from Dharamsala to one of the Tibetan schools the deception remains cruel, since at the moment there is no Tibetan school capable of providing an education which might compensate for the loss of an emotionally secure childhood.

The rider added by many parents to the effect that they wanted their children to be near His Holiness is doubtless a genuine personal feeling, and the Tibetan tradition of dedicating young children to the monasteries must make it easier to persuade parents to hand over their sons and daughters to a camp run by His Holiness's sister. Yet our observations here during the past few months show that family feeling is very strong among the Tibetans and it's difficult to believe that they would acquiesce to such a ruthless destruction of home-life unless thoroughly brainwashed by interested parties.

The fact that seventy-one out of seventy-three parents expressed willingness to have their children's futures organized by His Holiness does not now shock or surprise me as it would once have done. The fundamental problem posed by this attitude is none of our business and must be sorted out among the Tibetans themselves; one can only hope that they get it sorted out quickly, before the whole structure of their exiled society collapses.

It is interesting to speculate about the motives behind the Tibetan Government's urge to collect the maximum number of Tiblets in Dharamsala camp. Disregarding any possible financial inducements one is left with cultural and political motives. The Tibetan authorities themselves admit that when the camp was opened 'to shelter the children of refugees' physical needs were not the only consideration—it was also intended to shelter

these youngsters from un-Tibetan influences during their forma-
tive years. This ambition would be understandable if there were
even a sporting chance of the refugees returning to Tibet within
a decade or so, but in existing circumstances an exclusively
Tibetan preparation for a life that must be lived in the modern
world is unfair both to the children themselves and to those who
wish to help them re-settle; already there are too many examples
of the disastrous effects of suddenly transplanting adolescent
Tibetans into Western soil. However desirable the 'preservation'
of Tibetan culture may be some degree of integration is essential and the best and simplest way of achieving it would be to
allow as many children as possible to grow up in the Tibetan
atmosphere of their own families, without artificially protecting
them from the outside world.

Concerning the political implications it is just conceivable
that certain members of the Tibetan Government do envisage
the future invasion of Tibet by an Army of Liberation recruited
from amongst the refugee children. But it seems more probable
that the ruling clique (excluding the Dalai Lama) finds it
psychologically impossible to relinquish its power over the
people and is afraid that the new generation, if permitted to
grow up in an alien environment, will rapidly become emanci-
pated citizens of India.

It's not easy to be rational on this subject. One dreads the
evolution of a generation of rootless Tibetans, deprived of what
was, in its native air, a happy and healthy way of life. Yet one
also recognizes that this way of life is now extinct within Tibet
and that it is quite impractical to attempt to continue it outside
Tibet. The paradox is that a theocracy-cum-autocracy, when
seen against a democratic background, immediately antagon-
izes even those who admit that in its original context this was an
acceptable form of government. So I find myself at one moment
castigating the Tibetan authorities and at the next moment
trying to excuse their high-handed actions on the grounds that
it is unreasonable to expect them to have adjusted so soon to
their new environment.

A very regrettable feature of the Tibetan problem is that
most foreign aid has been administered in a way which rein-
forces the Tibetan Government's policy of splitting families.

The relief agencies seem to have started from the premise that under existing conditions it is impossible for children to remain with their parents, and the majority of operations have been conducted accordingly. It's probably inevitable that when a refugee crisis suddenly occurs the initial administration of aid should be a trifle haphazard—but one feels that order could come out of chaos rather more quickly than it's doing in this instance. Having taken a wrong turning at the beginning, through failure to investigate ways of keeping families united, the agencies seem determined consistently to follow the wrong road. As a result money that could have been spent on mobile medical and educational units is now being irretrievably sunk in the acquiring and staffing of permanent centres where hundreds of children can be cared for in the future—thus making it progressively more difficult to restore the balance of the whole Tibetan Community.

The agencies' original assumption that Tiblets must be cared for in large centres is a classic example of the dangers of applying Western standards to Eastern situations. Life in the road-camps is undoubtedly arduous, and the children who remain in them are exposed to the occasional risk of being injured by falling rocks during the blasting operations. It is unlikely that the average Western child would survive such conditions for long, and so the relief workers raise their hands in horror and decide that as many Tiblets as possible must be rescued as soon as possible. Yet if one pauses to think the thing out it soon becomes obvious that what we regard as the insupportable existence of a road-camp community is not unlike everyday life in Tibet. Many of the refugees came from nomad tribes who habitually lived in tents, and all of them were accustomed to some degree of hardship. The Indian Government pays the refugees a slightly higher wage than that of the native coolie, to compensate them for having no little plot on which to grow food, so a husband and wife can earn between them Rs. 22.75 (about £1 16s.) per seven-day week. By local standards this is quite a good wage and should enable the parents to feed their children much better than they are fed here—especially if some of the Indian Government per capita monthly food ration were distributed among the camps rather than sent in bulk to

ı

Dharamsala and other centres. The children's health could not possibly be worse anywhere than it is here, and while it may be true that some of our Tiblets would have died if not brought within reach of Western medical aid this does not invalidate the argument that in general these children would be far better off, both physically and emotionally, if they had not been parted from their parents.

It is ironical—and a symptom of the mental confusion in Tibetan Government circles—that the efforts being made to 'keep young Tibetans Tibetan' are in fact weakening the social structure of the whole refugee community. The damage done to children by separating them from their parents is no greater than the damage done to parents by relieving them of their natural responsibilities and one hears that in some areas this form of 'aid' has by now had a seriously demoralizing effect.

The intangible difficulties of assisting refugees are far more numerous and complicated than the difficulties of providing food and clothing. Every social worker's ideal is—or should be— 'to help them to help themselves', but this is not easily realized since the mere fact of having been so savagely uprooted by fate often predisposes refugees to take it for granted that those who have not suffered as they have will look after them. In fact workers with wide experience remark on the Tibetans being less prone than most to take things for granted; but obviously they present their own particular problems and it is extremely rash of any relief agency to plunge into the centre of a new refugee situation without having first paused on the outskirts to study its complexities.

In the Tibetans' case their malleability, when they are tact-fully handled, makes the foreign helper keenly aware of the importance of his role as their guide to a new world. The adjective 'simple' is frequently applied to these people, yet their national character is repeatedly surprising me by its contradictions. Though the average Tibetan is in many respects a very conservative fellow he can at times be frighteningly receptive to new ideas. This trait partly explains his adaptability but, since his powers of discrimination are usually undeveloped, it is potentially very dangerous. Therefore it seems wickedly foolish of us to help foster the notion that once a child is weaned it can automatically become someone else's responsibility.

13 NOVEMBER

During the past week Macleod Ganj has been transformed into a vast open-air Tibetan market where hundreds of pilgrims, who came for the recent religious festival, are now trading vigorously. Fabulous cloaks, hats, boots, rugs, swords, knives, jewellery and reliquaries are on display—and also other more significant, if less exotic, items of merchandise. On my first visit to this market I was a little (but only a little) startled to observe the variety of medicaments which were available at bargain prices. Bottles of eight Acromycin capsules were selling at Rs. 6, as compared to Rs. 10.50 in any chemist's shop. Bottles of fifty Zymacaps, clearly marked—'Donated by the Upjohn Foundation. Not for sale or exchange', were going for Rs. 5. Rolls of English manufactured Johnson and Johnson cotton wool were evidently more highly prized and cost Rs. 8; doubtless these were part of a large consignment sent from Britain last March and never heard of since. The traders were most anxious to sell me pills, and the fact that they drew the attention of a Western medical helper to these wares proves how incredibly innocent they are. This evening I again visited the market, taking an interpreter with me, and when I asked where these goods had come from the traders beamed happily and explained that during the summer a Tibetan from Dharamsala had gone up the Kulu valley selling them in the road-camps. I next asked what complaints the pills were used for and got the inevitable reply that they cured every disease immediately. It really is disheartening: I wonder what percentage of help donated to refugees all over the world 'goes astray'. Of course I could have pressed for the name of the 'Tibetan from Dharamsala' and then rushed off to the police barracks exuding righteous wrath, but after spending a few months in India one ceases to think in terms of reporting thefts to the police.

Another side-effect of last week's pilgrimage has been the infestation of the area by an inordinate number of Febs and Fabs, accompanied by an equal number of young Mebs and

Mabs. In this case I feel that the male of the species is deadlier than the female. A few days ago Oliver and I were standing by the bungalow door, waiting for lunch to be served, when we suddenly saw an extraordinary creature advancing towards us across the compound. It had red-gold ringlets halfway down its back, a wavy matching beard, delicate pink cheeks and corn-flower-blue eyes—and it was clad in a long, white Biblical robe. The net result was so like an inferior artist's conception of Christ that Oliver and I simultaneously exclaimed, 'Jesus!' Juliet, sitting behind us, thought that we'd both become un-characteristically blasphemous—but when this vision entered the room she saw what we meant.

These young enthusiasts have a tendency to roam around the camp performing esoteric tests to determine whether any of our Tiblets are Incarnate Lamas. This afternoon I was immensely diverted by one such test. As I was tapping a pneumonia case, with a solemn-faced four-year-old sitting on my left, staring into space—and Cama Yishy, as ever, sitting on my right—a group of Febs, Fabs, Mebs and Mabs appeared on the scene, surveyed the four-year-old and declared—'He seems *very* prob-able.' They then asked me if I'd noticed anything unusual about the child and I replied—'Yes, last month it had three different types of worms at the same time.' Whereupon they all looked quite revolted—whether by the medical fact or by my insensi-tive obtuseness I wouldn't know. Next they proceeded to squat around in a semi-circle, waving their hands and muttering 'mantras' and making profound deductions from the infant's understandably astonished reactions. Finally they announced— 'This boy is a most interesting case and we must tell our "Guru" that he Shows All The Signs.' This was the cue I'd been devil-ishly waiting for. 'Yes,' I said, 'we all know it's an interesting case—but I hardly think your "Guru" would thank you for bringing him to investigate an Incarnate Lama who is in fact a girl.'


15 November

A horrible incident occurred this morning. Each day after breakfast I take our left-overs—bread, cheese and hard-boiled egg—to the Dispensary for distribution among those who most need 'feeding up'. Normally the food is wrapped in a piece of newspaper but to-day, being in a rush and seeing none to hand, I hurried across the compound with the food exposed on a plate. Before I was half-way across a mob of starving children had brought me to a standstill. Suddenly Tibetan gentleness was replaced by a barbarous aggressiveness. Panic filled me as I looked around at the mass of struggling little bodies, in the midst of which some tiny ones were falling and being trampled underfoot. This was genuine mob violence, appearing in the most unlikely place, and it was horrifying to see the expression of frantically pleading desperation in those young eyes. The ayahs must have been at their breakfast, for none answered my calls, and as Juliet had preceded me to the Dispensary the only way to quell this riot was to throw bits of food in various directions, thereby splitting up the mob into groups. The whole experience was indescribably dreadful and I haven't yet forgiven myself for causing it through sheer thoughtlessness. Of course we've always known that the children are inadequately fed, but somehow when you see them sitting down to four meals per diem you don't realize that they are literally starving: and probably the recent cold weather is largely responsible for their present state of agonizing hunger.

Our working day now ends at 5 p.m. because the evenings are so cold and dark. The children have supper then and are in bed by half-past five—a rather dismal arrangement, but in unheated draughty rooms there's no alternative.

This evening I went to the Drama for the tenth time; these plays seem more enjoyable the more familiar they become. When I set off for the 'theatre' soon after five o'clock the valley was filled with golden evening light and the cool, clear air was deliciously exhilarating. As usual I was on the alert for possible zoological excitements, and half-way to Macleod Ganj I saw what at first appeared to be two squirrels, playing in a giant pine-tree a little distance from the track. When I went closer to investigate they ran up to the topmost branches and it became obvious that they were not squirrels. As they watched me the setting sun shone magnificently on their glossy chestnut backs and when I sat quietly near the tree I saw that they had ginger bellies and coal-black tips to their very bushy tails, which were as long as their bodies. (Nose to tail-tip they measured about three feet and they were short legged, with small round ears and ferrety faces.) After ten minutes or so they apparently decided that I was harmless and began to play again, approaching to within five yards of me. Then I noticed the very loose folds of skin between their fore and hind legs and at last realized that they were flying foxes. To see them gliding I deliberately chased them up the tree and they took off from the top branch and sailed slowly downwards for about thirty yards before coming to rest in the lower branches of another pine. I followed them and this graceful performance was thrice repeated—by which time the path was far behind, darkness was falling and I suddenly remembered that bears as well as flying foxes inhabit the forest. At this stage my torch battery gave out, so during the remainder of the walk to the theatre I expected to meet a bear at every corner and was quite hoarse from singing arias. For the return journey I joined a group of ayahs and we all sang together as we marched along the starlit road.

16 NOVEMBER

Bad as material conditions were when I first arrived in this camp, the past fortnight has been by far the most depressing period of my time here. Parents who came on the pilgrimage are now returning to their road-camps and day after day we see families being broken up—wherever one turns one glimpses a weeping parent or a sobbing child. To-day I witnessed a particularly harrowing scene, when a family which has just come from Tibet—the journey took them fourteen months—reluctantly abandoned seven of their eight children; only the six-months-old baby stayed with its mother. She was a handsome woman of thirty-four with two husbands—the elder thirty-nine and the younger thirty-one. The eldest child is a ten-year-old boy and there are four-year-old twin girls. All the children— except a three-year-old boy with bronchitis—are in perfect health, despite what must have been a most gruelling journey. I wonder how long their health will remain perfect, now that they have been submerged in Dharamsala camp.

These people are nomads who have never slept under a roof and who speak a dialect that only one man here can understand—not because he is a native of their locality, but because as a Lhasa Government official he was posted for a time to the relevant area of Western Tibet. With his assistance I discovered that they had attempted to bring their herd of 200 sheep and goats with them, but of course when crossing those barren heights of the Himalayas, where for days on end there is no fodder of any sort, the unfortunate animals quickly died of starvation. This misfortune is common to many refugee families and it explains their utter destitution on arriving in India. One could be quite well-off in Tibet without possessing any cash; wealth was often represented entirely by livestock.

I shall never forget the hysterical grief of that family when the time came for the parents to go. The mother fondled all her children, said good-bye and turned away—but then turned back again and was almost pulled to the ground by seven panic-stricken little pairs of arms. Finally her husbands—big raw-boned men with weather-blackened faces—took her firmly but very gently in charge and though weeping openly themselves led her away down the mountain-side. This parting took place in Kashmir Cottage Room, where there are two doors and where I was in sole charge, all the ayahs having gone to Macleod Ganj to collect stores. As soon as the parents were out of sight the seven children dashed to the doors to follow them—the twins to one door, the rest to the other. I rushed to intercept the larger party and bolt that door while Cama Yishy, on his own initiative, headed off the twins from their exit, and though he could not reach the bolt he shut the door and bravely defended his post. When the children realized that they were trapped in this vast, unfamiliar cavern they went berserk. The phrase 'going up the walls' literally did apply to three of them, who tried piteously to claw their way up the smooth boards to the high windows. Another hurled herself against a door in such a paroxysm of panic that I feared that she would bash her brains out. And the twins lay kicking on the floor and shrieked with terror when I approached them—not surprisingly, since they had probably never seen a European face before. Meanwhile Cama Yishy had taken it on himself to console the three-year-old, who was crouching in the corner, whimpering with fear, and as I stood helplessly in the centre of that room I vowed to do all in my power, from this day on, to alter a situation that creates so much misery.

It was illuminating that when being questioned on their arrival as to why they had brought their children here these parents gave the stock answer—'Because they will get schooling and it is good for them to be near His Holiness.' Yet in Tibet this family lived four months' journey by horse from Lhasa and had never been there or seen the Dalai Lama. (My question-naire has shown me that few Tibetans, except those living in nearby towns and villages, ever went to the capital.) As for education, it is utterly beyond the bounds of possibility that such people, who don't even speak Tibetan, could have thought this one out for themselves—so it seems justifiable to assume that during the three days which they have just spent in Forsythe Bazaar they were thoroughly indoctrinated.

Admittedly it is best under present conditions that at least some of the children, in a case like this, should be left at a camp while their parents find work; the tragedy is that even when work has been found the family will not be encouraged to re-unite.

This afternoon I had a most enjoyable row with Umadevi, an elderly Polish-born Feb who lives at the Palace. She accused me of being bigoted, conceited and treacherous, and I accused her of being fanatical, jealous and totally incapable of seeing the realities of any situation. After two and three-quarter hours of such exchanges we parted the best of friends—possible because we both found that quarrelling with each other, rather than with Mrs Tsiring Dolma, was a truly satisfying experience. Certainly I felt that having someone saying what they thought of me to my face made a very nice change.

In the course of our conversation—if the interview may be so described—Umadevi asked petulantly, 'Why don't all you foreigners go back to your own countries and look after affairs there, instead of interfering with the Tibetans?' To me this was a delectable question, coming from a Pole who has spent the past three years virtually running the Tibetan Government Foreign Affairs Department. I said as much, to which my opponent replied that *she* was only trying to help—whereupon I retorted that it was a matter of opinion whether 'help' or 'interference' was the *mot juste* for any of our activities. She then went on to accuse me of being 'like the C.I.D.'—a charge which left me completely uninsulted because, as I pointed out, C.I.D.s are necessary evils, human nature being what it is. As can be seen, our meeting was not exactly productive, except in so far as it gave us both the opportunity to let off a great deal of long-pent-up steam. I only wish that I was more deserving of comparison with the C.I.D.—though actually Interpol is what we need here.

The walk to the Palace is more beautiful than ever at this season and when returning westward at sunset, as I did to-day, one is confronted by a vast red-gold sky, smouldering behind the dark, deep green of the forests. To the south lie long, multi-coloured streamers of cloud against a pale, cold green sky and near-by hundreds of almond trees are richly blossoming among the pines and deodars. Occasionally too one notices a strangely lovely tree whose transparent leaves have now turned to the palest gold and adding to this beauty is the unceasing music of the Tibetan flute. All day, from dawn to dusk, wherever you go in this region, you hear that flute being played in the distance; yet never once have I *seen* it being played, which makes me feel that it's the original 'music of the spheres'—an illusion fostered by the quiet, simple tunes.

It's hateful to think that within a fortnight I'll have left this glorious region and returned to the plains.

## 23 NOVEMBER

It has taken us all day to realize that President Kennedy is dead. We heard of the assassination at 8 a.m. on the Delhi news, and though India had her own national tragedy yesterday (when five of her senior army and air force officers were killed in a helicopter crash not very far from here) three-quarters of the bulletin was devoted to Kennedy. The Russian tribute struck us as being sincere, and if this impression is correct its sincerity is the best epitaph he could have. It is curious how hostile feelings to the American way of life and policies do not prevent most Westerners from involuntarily regarding the President of the United States as *our* leader—not merely the leader of a friendly power. At least that's how the four of us here—representing three European nations—reacted this morning. There was a sense of personal loss in our sorrow—and also an element of fear, at being suddenly deprived of a protector whose individual greatness had placed him outside the area of petty international antagonisms, while his humanity kept him within reach of the least of us.

This evening President Radhakrishnan broadcast a tribute and the most impressive thing about it was its incoherency. Last month I mentioned his fine talk on the eve of U.N. Day, when every idea was carefully thought out and perfectly expressed; but to-day he spoke very slowly and haltingly and it was the tone of his voice, rather than the inevitable *clichés*, that said what he felt.

The 'apartness' of the Tibetans is heavily underlined by this tragedy. To them 'America' and 'Kennedy' are meaningless words, and the recent death of the camp dog affected them much more deeply than the assassination of an unknown statesman. This fact, when they have now been living in India for four years, proves how effective a language barrier is—and also how little the average adult refugee is interested in his new environment. It's unlikely that there are any other people—apart from primitive tribes in inaccessible areas—to whom to-day's news meant nothing.

Last night the camp suffered a slight crisis when Pema, a five-year-old girl who had been left here by her mother yesterday afternoon, was found to have disappeared. At about 9 p.m. an unprecedented commotion started up outside the bungalow and on investigating we learned that a search party was being formed. I felt certain that in these forests, at this season, the poor little scrap couldn't possibly survive—but here I underestimated the toughness of Tiblets. Half an hour after the search party had set out a messenger who had gone to Macleod Ganj to notify the mother came rushing back with the news that Pema had made her own way to the hamlet, walking over two miles in pitch darkness, and that she was now asleep, safely snuggled down beside her 'amela' in sheepskins by the roadside. She was not brought back here to-day, as I feared she might be, so perhaps her gallant escape-march has had the desired effect.

## 26 NOVEMBER

This is my last day on duty in the camp and now I wish I was gone; within the past week my happiness, on going out each morning and being inundated by a wave of Tiblets, has turned to bitterness at the thought of leaving. It is difficult to understand, much less explain, what these children have done for me. All I know is that during the past four months they have caused a subtle but powerful transformation, so that I'm aware of taking something away from here that will be of permanent value. To those who have never lived through such an experience my words may sound like so much sentimental tommy-rot —yet they express a reality which others have already observed. Yesterday, Oliver slightly startled me by remarking on how much I had changed since we first met. When I asked him how this change looked to him he replied without hesitation—'In some ways you're softer and in other ways you're much stronger and calmer.' I knew exactly what he meant and in fact I was able to return this compliment sincerely, for he too has been noticeably influenced by life among the Tiblets.

Two days ago the Simla Land-Rover appeared again, this time bringing Stuart and Miss Doris Betts and Deirdre Allen, the nineteen-year-old V.S.O. worker who is replacing me. Deirdre has been helping at the Manor since last July and is a tremendous character, remarkably mature for her years and tough enough to take even Dharamsala camp in her stride. Yet she is also very gentle and full of fun and has the perfect temperament for looking after Tiblets; within a day of her arrival she had become 'one of the lads' and it was obvious that every child in the place—including Cama Yishy—already adored her. This is an indescribable relief to me, for Tiblets are philosophical little creatures, not likely to be upset by a change of staff when the new 'Amela' is capable of giving them at least as much understanding affection as the old.

Miss Betts is matron of the Manor Nursery for Tibetan Refugee Children, and she came with Stuart on this trip to help him select another batch of weakly Tiblets for transfer to Simla. Originally we had planned to leave here to-day, but as poor Stuart has again got bogged down in the morass of Mrs Tsiring Dolma's obstructiveness our departure has been postponed till to-morrow.

My plans for the immediate future are as follows: to leave Roz here and go to Simla by Land-Rover; to hitch-hike from there to Delhi, do some Christmas shopping for Juliet and get Nepalese visas for Doris and Oliver, who are both taking well-earned holidays next month; to return to Dharamsala by rail and bus, say final good-byes and then cycle up the Kulu valley to see for myself what life is like in the road-camps.

To-day I found that the last remnants of my patience with Mrs Tsiring Dolma had frayed away to nothing—perhaps because the need for diplomacy on my part is now over. I happened to be in the Dispensary this morning when a ten-year-old girl from the Upper Nursery was brought to Oliver suffering from such advanced gingivitis that every one of her teeth was loose and her gums were like crimson jelly. The weather is now bitterly cold yet this child was clad in a thin, torn, sleeveless cotton frock—though when V.I.P.s visit the Upper Nursery every child there is dressed warmly in tweeds, woollens, heavy socks and strong boots.

Half an hour afterwards, while I was still seething with wrath, a message came from Mrs Tsiring Dolma saying that she expected Deirdre and me at a luncheon party to be given in our honour at the Upper Nursery. These invitations to ritual luncheons always come in the form of Royal Commands and the only acceptable excuse for declining them is serious illness. However I declined, as I have done twice before with thanks but without offering any excuse; had I been pressed to explain my reasons for not attending to-day it would have given me great pleasure to point out that twelve-course luncheons for the favoured few do not impress guests who are aware of the presence in this camp of hundreds of hungry children. This morning Stuart also declined his invitation, being equally opposed to these lavish parties. By now he had given up attempting to make Mrs Tsiring Dolma see reason on the various points under discussion and at 12.30 p.m. we set off together to climb to

Triund Rest House, which is perched on a mountain ridge at a height of 10,300 feet. I've got so completely out of training that I found this trek very tiring—especially as Stuart is an exceptionally athletic type who sets a terrific pace. But it was well worth the effort, to see so much wild beauty on every side, and I returned feeling much the better for the expedition.

Yesterday, while instructing Deirdre in her new duties, I suddenly realized that the number of infected ears in the Lower Nursery is now down to 36, as compared with 315 a few months ago, and these simple statistics gave me a more glowing sense of achievement than I have ever felt before. They also prove that in this sort of situation every helper, however inexperienced, can significantly contribute to the relief of suffering.

# 8

## *Here and There*

The impersonality of refugee work struck me very forcibly this morning when we were preparing our nine chosen Tiblets for the long journey to Simla. At 5 a.m. three ayahs arrived at the bungalow carrying or leading their sleepy-eyed charges, who were put on Juliet's bed and told to be good. Then the ayahs quietly disappeared and that was the abrupt ending of one chapter in these young lives. Their unquestioning acceptance of this upheaval seemed pathetic: it would have been easier to cope with fits of alarmed weeping than to witness such calm indifference. I couldn't help wondering what this change would mean for each of them. One at least was being parted from a brother; another has a father living in Macleod Ganj, who will probably lose track of her as she moves from camp to camp, and as for the rest—months may pass before their parents learn of this transfer. Yet to everyone in authority these are no more than nine numbers to be crossed off the Dharamsala register and entered on the Simla register.

Within an hour Miss Betts had achieved a miracle of organization. All nine Tiblets were securely tucked up in comfortable 'beds' in the back of the Land-Rover, countless flasks had been filled with hot milk, provision had been made for dealing quickly and efficiently with bouts of car-sickness and diarrhœa and a picnic lunch had been packed for us.

The 206-mile journey along precipitous, winding roads took us exactly twelve hours, yet one couldn't wish for the trip to end. Our route lay through the Himalayan foothills—which anywhere else would be referred to as majestic mountains—and these vast, lonely sweeps of earth and sky seemed intoxicating in the crystal air.

Even after living among Tiblets for four months I was astonished by our passengers' behaviour; not once did one of them so much as whimper. At each of the three stops we lifted them out, asked them to 'chimbathombhi'—which they obligingly did, squatting in a row by the wayside—fed them with milk and rusks, repacked them and then set off again.

It was dark when we arrived here and though Simla is such an uninspiring place by day the approach by night is quite breathtakingly beautiful. The sheer slopes glow from their very summits down to the valleys' depths with tens of thousands of sparkling lights; when you come round the mountain and see this sight ahead it looks as though some hoard of diamonds has been spilled out of the sky.

After sharing quarters for so long it's an extraordinary sensation to sit here tonight in the solitude of the Menteths' guest-room. But even the priceless blessing of privacy doesn't outweigh the loneliness. However, it's nice to look forward to going to bed now under an open window, with the icy wind blowing on my face. And here, at 7,000 feet above sea level, it *is* icy!

## SIMLA: 28 NOVEMBER

Having finished the above at 11.30 p.m. I retired under my open window—but at 1 a.m. I was still tossing and turning. Eventually the penny dropped; after four months of 'sleeping hard' my body simply couldn't relax on a soft bed. I then migrated with blankets to the floor and a moment later had fallen fast asleep.

The weather was so appalling here to-day that the prospect of going down to the plains has become quite attractive. All morning a ferocious north wind tore around this summit, flaying it with sleet, and after lunch Simla had its first snowfall of the season. At tea-time I went over to the Manor to see The Nine, who all looked very happy—but how I should hate to work at either of these S.C.F. nurseries! For all its faults, snags, hardships and hazards Dharamsala does provide Tiblets with some passable substitute for their natural habitat and to see them here, being briskly Europeanized within twenty-four hours of arrival, has a most depressing effect on me. Yet material conditions in these nurseries are so much better than in Dharamsala that the eight Dispensary cases who were transferred three weeks ago have already improved beyond recognition; I would never have been able to pick them out if they hadn't rushed to welcome 'Amela'.

Clearly a compromise is required between the comfort of Simla and the squalor of Dharamsala. The expenditure of comparatively large sums on maintaining these palatial, English-type homes for a mere 300 children, when so many other hundreds are neglected elsewhere, shows just how rotten things are in the State of Tibland. S.C.F.'s approach gives the impression that those who direct the operation from London are intent on upholding the highest British standards of comfort, cleanliness and kindly regimentation, regardless of their suitability in a particular context. And one of the most frustrating aspects of this situation is that the available field-workers have a very firm grasp of the realities of the problem and could efficiently implement a more constructive project if given the opportunity. Surely such intelligent and enterprising helpers should be free to work out, from their own observations on the spot, the best way of organizing relief.

### New Delhi: 2 December

Having left Simla at 9 a.m. on the 29th, I arrived here in Delhi at 4 a.m. next day, after an uneventful journey in a series of trucks driven by polite Sikhs. In India the picking up of hitch-hikers is one of a truck-driver's 'perks' and, for a fraction of what the bus-fare would cost, villagers travel long distances adhering to the tops of the most improbable loads. Being a white woman I got preferential treatment and was accommodated in the cab, though in fact it is illegal for drivers to give lifts to foreigners.

During the past few days Jill and I have spent most of our time together, discussing Tibbery and visiting innumerable offices concerned with the relief of the refuges. To-morrow morning I'm going by bus to Mussoorie, bringing some medical supplies to the Schools and Homes there.

### Mussoorie: 6 December

On Tuesday morning Jill drove me to the bus-station at 5 a.m.

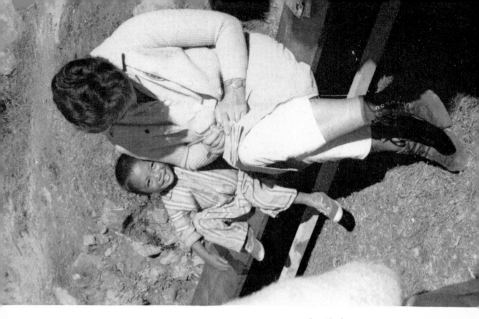

The author
with Cama
Yishy

Thondup Tsing
with Bran

Getting ready to
go from Forsythe
Bazaar

The author and
Roz on the road
again

and by four o'clock that afternoon I was back on the heights among Tiblets.

It's odd how quickly one adjusts to the tremendous distances involved in travelling around India; despite the thirteen-hour journey I found myself quite naturally thinking of Mussoorie as being 'near Delhi'!

For many miles the road runs north across an apparently endless grey-brown plain where sugar-cane is the main crop; only on approaching Dehra Dun does the landscape change to heavily wooded hills. Here one transfers to a local bus and for the next twenty-two miles up to Mussoorie the madly cork-screwing road seems like an entertainment in a giant's fun-fair.

Throughout Tibland the word 'Mussoorie' is now synonymous with 'Taring'—a name which was familiar too in old Tibet, where this family ranked high among the nobility. Jigme Sum-chen Wang-po Namgyal Taring was an army officer for about twelve years before becoming Treasurer to the Tibetan Government. He is first cousin to the Maharaja of Sikkim and this week is away in Gangtok at the funeral of his uncle, the late Maharaja. His wife, Rinchin Dolma Taring, wrote to me recently and I quote now from her letter.

My husband was guarding His Holiness's Palace along with the other Tibetan Officials during the uprising in Tibet. He had no time to go back home when Lhasa got shelled and he followed His Holiness by the same track and ever since he has been serving as a Principal of the Tibetan Refugee School, Mussoorie. As for myself; I was also not at home during the uprising in Tibet and also left Tibet by myself through Bhutan. I used to serve the Women's Association in Tibet. When I came to India through God's kindness, I was lucky enough to be able to unite with my husband in Darjeeling. When I first came to India, I went to Kalimpong, where I helped our young Tibetans to learn English, and later on I was asked to come to Mussoorie to help my husband to run the School, and at the end of 1962, His Holiness asked me to organize the Tibetan Children's Homes and I had this great opportunity of serving these children to whom I have completely dedicated myself.

K

After my wearing and disillusioning encounters with Tibetan officials in Dharamsala it was heartening to meet Mrs Taring, see the work which she and her husband are doing and realize that there *is* a brighter side to the Tibetan aristocracy. Mussoorie is a place where everyone works together in harmony, no money is 'mislaid' and no goods 'go astray'. (Perhaps this is why it is not a popular project among some of the relief agencies in Delhi; when dealing with the Tarings it is impossible to come to 'an arrangement for mutual benefit'.)

The Tibetan Homes Foundation consists of some twenty houses and bungalows, which have been bought or rented with foreign aid. Each of these accommodates twenty-five boys and girls, under the care of Tibetan House-Parents, and here at last I have found that compromise between luxury and squalor which I mentioned the other day. In all the homes one sees happy, healthy children—but standards have been kept at a reasonable level. The manner in which Mrs Taring has organized this whole project proves that when the right type of Tibetan takes responsibility the refugees themselves are best fitted to cope with their own problems.

At the Mussoorie Tibetan Refugee School, run by Mr Taring, 600 boarders live in two huge hostels and are joined for lessons by most of the 500 children from the Homes. The education available here is no better than elsewhere, but that is not the Tarings' fault; until this whole question is approached from a different angle no individual can do anything to improve the situation. Meanwhile these 600 boys and girls are being adequately clothed and fed and kept in contact with the best ingredients of their own culture.

Mussoorie is by far the most impressive of the relief schemes, yet it provides no satisfactory long-term solution; in fact its existence could ultimately have a bad effect if parents are encouraged, by Western workers, to regard it as a permanent feature of refugee life.

I'm staying here with the S.C.F. nurse, Miss Joan Ariel, who runs a small, well-equipped Dispensary which, as in Dharamsala, is also used as a hospital. To me it seemed incredible to find only thirteen patients there, not one of whom would have been considered ill enough for admission to our Dispensary.

New Delhi: 9 December

On Saturday I left Miss Ariel's bungalow at 6 a.m., carrying thirty pounds of drugs not needed at Mussoorie but badly needed at Dharamsala. My personal luggage is never very bulky (it all fits in Roz's saddle-bag, detached and converted to a suit-case) and as I have by now perfected the coolie technique of carrying loads I arrived at the bus-station, four miles away, with no more than an aching shoulder. That really was a mag-nificent trek, begun in moonlight, continued while a glorious dawn briefly tinted the snow peaks to the north and ended as the first sunlight came pouring triumphantly over the mountains on to the limitless plain below. And, as I passed the various Homes, the early silence was being broken continually by groups of Tiblets singing their morning prayers, followed by the poignant Tibetan National Anthem.

The journey back here was not as boring as you might imagine from my previous description of the landscape; whatever other criticisms India may merit she is never dull. I have noticed too that since returning to the real India from Dharamsala I'm find-ing it much easier to come to terms with the country and the people. Perhaps my first impressions were prejudiced by heat-stroke in July—or possibly the Buddhist influence has made my reactions a little less intolerant. At any rate India no longer rubs me up the wrong way *all* the time and I'm very much en-joying these few days in Delhi.

Yesterday was Sunday so Jill and I foreswore Tibbery, and at 4 p.m. I set out to walk to the Gemini Circus grounds opposite the Red Fort in Old Delhi.

Circuses are among the more innocuous of my secret vices and this one was well worth the long wait, in a turbulent queue, for a cheap ticket. Not that queueing in these surroundings could ever be tedious. On my left lay the long, noble lines of the Red Fort and on my right the dull red stone of the massively delicate Jama Mosjid Mosque stood out against a tremendous glow of bronzed sunset clouds. Also, now that the necessary adjustment to India has been achieved, I revelled in this amalgamation with thousands of fellow queue-ers and in the whole noisy, glittering, pushing scene.

The show, which started punctually at 7 p.m., had everything
that a European circus has—but bigger and better. It was over
at 11 p.m. and then, before walking back to New Delhi through
the pleasantly keen night air, I had a supper of 'Kababs' and
new-baked bread in one of the many little Muslim eating-houses
that huddle in the shadow of the Jama Mosjid. In this Islamic
quarter of Delhi many of the women still go veiled and the cooking is reminiscent of Pakistan. It became noticeable here that
despite the inward truce between myself and Hinduism I still
find it very much easier to relax and feel at home among
Muslims.

My way back to the main thoroughfare led through a tangle
of ancient, narrow streets, which were strewn with sleeping
figures hidden in cocoons of threadbare blankets. At the end of
one of these alleyways the sound of a brass-band attracted my
attention and, suspecting a Hindu wedding, I paused to see the
fun. Soon the band appeared, about ten yards ahead of a magnificently caparisoned horse on which rode the bridegroom and
best-man. This animal was entirely covered in what seemed to
be a sort of gold-plated 'armour' and the bridegroom was clad
in elaborate robes and wore a high head-dress from which hung
a curtain of coloured beads, completely hiding his face. Immediately preceding the horse were two drummers and two spectac-
ularly attired dancers—adolescent boys disguised as girls. At
intervals the procession stopped and the drummers drummed
and the dancers danced and never have I seen anything to equal
this display of primitive frenzy. The drummers looked quite
crazed with the speed of their own playing, and as the dancers
approached the climax of their performance, with eyes staring,
mouths foaming and bodies writhing, one could almost believe
that they were deriving their passionate energy from some non-
human source.

As they turned into the next street I felt that this was a
glimpse of that India which we will never understand.

Perhaps I'm getting too emotionally involved in my work,
because I find it quite heartbreaking to walk along Janpath and
see the stalls where Tibetan silver is on display. Thousands of
refugees arrived in India so destitute that they were thankful to
sell for five or ten shillings articles worth fifty times that price,

and many traders—both Indian and Tibetan—quickly took advantage of the peasants' poverty and commercial innocence. So now prayer-wheels, reliquaries and jewellery are being sold at fancy prices to pop-eyed, laughing tourists and when one knows the spiritual and sentimental value of such articles to the Tibetans this spectacle is almost unbearable.

DHARAMSALA: 12 DECEMBER

Really it was foolish of me to return here for such a short period; the look of incredulous delight on Cama Yishy's face when I suddenly reappeared will haunt me for a long time to come. And my general 'welcome back' was unexpectedly overwhelming. From the edge of the compound, overlooking the road, a few Tiblets saw me approaching, and by the time I arrived the lot had been alerted; for all their tininess the combined force nearly killed me with hugs and I couldn't help wondering what I'd ever done to deserve such a demonstration.

The eleven-hour train journey from Delhi to Pathancot was my first experience of the legendary Indian railways—reputed to be the world's most interesting and exhausting form of transport. However, this was no baptism of fire, since the Kashmiri Express is naturally not popular in mid-Winter and even the third-class coaches were half-empty. I lay stretched on the wooden seat, using my saddle-bag as pillow, and slept for most of the time till we reached Pathancot at 8 a.m. this morning—though my responsibilities included all Juliet's Christmas shopping, plus Bran.

The saga of Bran is worth telling. Yesterday morning Jill and I were sitting in Arabella near Connaught Circus, discussing Tibbery, when suddenly Jill heard and saw a diminutive mongrel puppy being used as a football by a small Sikh boy. Instantly she was out of the Land-Rover and across the road—miraculously escaping a speeding Mercedes—and from the terrified expression on the small boy's face, before he collected his wits and fled out of sight, I can only deduce that she was looking positively homicidal. Having picked the trembling puppy out of the gutter she re-crossed the road, more prudently this time, and I wondered where we all went from here; Jill is already owned by a year-old variation on the Alsatian theme, which has been living in the back of Arabella since she rescued it three weeks ago, and her frantic efforts to find it a home have to date been unsuccessful.

When the latest waif and stray had been deposited on my lap I saw that he was about six weeks old, weighed some thirty ounces and had an utterly adorable personality. Jill said briskly, 'We'll have him put down this evening', and I said, 'Of course: absolutely no alternative'—both of us knowing full well that when evening came we would produce unimpeachable reasons for not being able to contact a veterinary surgeon. During the next half-hour the waif sat on my lap devouring Jill's protein biscuits—and then I announced that it was being named Bran, in honour of my deceased Irish terrier. Jill commented that naming the object was a poor beginning to the process of having it put down before nightfall, to which I retorted that feeding the object vastly expensive protein biscuits was an equally poor beginning to the same process. However, it was definite that Arabella had reached saturation point as far as dogs were concerned, so by 9 p.m. we had decided that some animal companionship would be very good psychological therapy for Tiblets— and Bran was put with my luggage.

Rather to my surprise he travelled like a veteran and was no bother, even doing what he was meant to do when held out of the window, as Indian mothers hold their babies at every stop. (Indian babies are not scarce, so this may be one reason why Indian stations have something in common with neglected farmyards.) He is now in the Dispensary, giving the children there a great deal of pleasure and enjoying life enormously. Obviously co-ordination is what's needed in this type of work!

### KANGRA: 18 DECEMBER

During the past six days I've been based on Dharamsala, while travelling around this area doing what Umadevi would doubtless describe as 'C.I.D. work'.

I finally left the camp to-day at 3 p.m., swathed in the

ceremonial white scarves presented by Tibetans on these occasions. All morning, while I oiled, washed and checked Roz, crowds of Tiblets had been surrounding me, staring in wonder at the strange machine. (For obvious reasons bicycles are not used in this area.) After lunch I cycled round the compound to demonstrate how the thing worked and gave rides to those brave enough to want them. Poor Dubkay got very envious then and begged to be allowed to cycle a little way down the road; but Roz is so much lighter and faster than the Indian models to which he was accustomed on the plains that I didn't dare risk him going over a precipice. Instead, I gave him a farewell present of my solar topi, which he immediately clapped on his head—despite the cold north wind—to the great joy of the assembled Tiblets. Finally my saddle-bag was packed and, saying as few good-byes as possible, I left the camp via a back route, escorted by Juliet, Oliver, Kesang, Deirdre and a number of ayahs. These accompanied me as far as Forsythe Bazaar, where dozens of the resident Tibetans joined the group. Then I mounted Roz—for the first time in five months—and a moment later we had whizzed away out of sight down the steep road.

It was a fortunate coincidence that my departure from Dharamsala meant a reunion with Roz; as we gathered speed I revelled in the comforting contact with her handlebars, in the familiar rush of sharp air past my face and in experiencing once again the thrill of judging the maximum speed at which we could safely take hair-pin bends.

A few miles before reaching Kangra we passed the junction where to-morrow morning we'll be turned east towards Kulu and looking up the narrow road I felt that sudden racing of the pulse which is my personal symptom of wanderlust. Our overland journey from Ireland had assuaged it temporarily, but now it was rampant again and I almost trembled with impatience to be away over those splendidly mountainous horizons. The nomadic existence in which one never knows what may befall between dawn and dusk—or where one will find a bed when dusk has come—is a very essential ingredient in my life.

My bed here in Kangra is Spartan enough to satisfy the most

exacting nomad. I'm staying with the Canadian University Service Overseas Volunteers at the Kangra Boys' School, sleeping in blankets on a rotten wood floor whose days (and presumably nights) are very definitely numbered. Also I've just been warned not to register alarm and despondency if the mammoth rats who share this accommodation with the girls should chance to scuttle across my face during the small hours.

It's remarkable how Tibbery tends to attract extremes; the numbers of heroes and villains met with in Tibland make me feel at times that I'm living within a Victorian melodrama. These twenty-two-year-old C.U.S.O. volunteers—Lois James, a nurse, and Judy Pullen, a teacher—could each be earning high salaries in Canada if they had not chosen to come here for two years and live in unimaginable squalor on an allowance of one and sixpence *per diem*. Since their arrival in October they've visited us occasionally at Dharamsala, and from our first meeting I admired them enormously, both for their rapid adaptation to the complexities of life in Tibland and for the courage, resourcefulness and humour with which they were tackling their jobs. But now, having seen the conditions under which they live, the food on which they subsist and the incredible improvements they have made during two brief months no words seem adequate to praise them. When I think of the comparative luxury of Dharamsala, where the S.C.F. bungalow almost attains Western standards of comfort and where we lived royally on our S.C.F. food bonus, I feel deeply ashamed of the fact that some people regard me as having endured a martyr's existence for the sake of the Tiblets. Judy and Lois seem to be tough young women— Lois has already spent eighteen months living with the Esquimaux in the Canadian Arctic—but Kangra is a far less healthy spot than Dharamsala and on their present regime of too much work and too little food it is almost inevitable that they will succumb to one—or several—of the virulent local bugs.

When I arrived here at dusk we all walked up to the Maple Leaf Hospital and I said good-bye to Dr Haslem and her staff, who all do a great deal to help the Tibetans, though they are permanently overworked in their own jobs.

On our way back to the school the girls went on a mild shopping spree in the bazaar, using a small gift of money recently sent them from home to buy little presents for distribution during the Christmas party they are now planinng to give their Tiblets. It was fun to wander through the narrow streets, lit only by lanterns shining from the many little stalls, and to stop for long debates on the comparative values of fourpenny combs, threepenny tin whistles and vivid glass bangles at six for twopence-halfpenny. It has sometimes been remarked to me that Canadians are in general more adaptable than Americans, and certainly these two girls fit effortlessly into the Indian scene. Rarely have I seen Westerners display, in their dealings with Indians, such an unselfconscious and total acceptance of the equality of man.

Inevitably Judy and Lois urged me to spend Christmas at Kangra. Juliet and Deirdre had already urged me to spend it at Dharamsala and it's rather obvious that my disappearance into the wilds of Kulu at this season is regarded as an irreligious and anti-social idiosyncrasy. But to me an escape from all the nostalgic Christmas ritual and paraphernalia seems excellent psychology when home is five thousand miles away.

# 9

## Camping with Tibetans

MANDI: 20 DECEMBER

Roz and I left Kangra at ten o'clock yesterday morning and
took it very easy. Apart from the dysentery which has been
plaguing me this past week—so that my diet consists mainly of
sulphaguanidine tablets and my energy is proportionately reduced—cycling muscles sieze up during a five months' 'layoff'
and even the freewheel down from Dharamsala had made me
slightly saddle-sore. So I planned to cover only the twenty-
seven miles to Palampur where the four Peace Corps boys, who
have been based there since September, had invited me to stay
the night. Actually when we arrived in Palampur at 3 p.m.
I still felt quite fresh, having slept for over an hour in the sun,
and the temptation to go further was strong; but I resisted it,
knowing what agony over-doing things to-day could cause by
tomorrow.

It's difficult to describe the perfection of the weather here at
this season. There's nothing quite like it in Ireland, but the
nearest would be a clear, sunny, late September day. The visibility is fantastic now: a few days ago I could distinctly see
Simla from the heights above the Nursery.

The current Indian custom of measuring distances by both
miles and kilometres imposes a severe mental strain on travellers
with no flair for arithmetic. Every other signpost or milestone
uses a different measure and to add to the confusion English is
now being replaced by Hindi, a move which has been universally acknowledged as a specially pure form of lunacy. Almost
everyone who can read Hindi can also read English and most
citizens can read neither—so why take it out on the unfortunate
foreign traveller? It seems absurd that both scripts can't be
used, as Pakistan uses Urdu and English and as we use Gaelic
and English. The Government intend soon to replace English

by Hindi as India's official language and this is bound to worsen the already formidable chaos of Indian bureaucracy. Even in the military sphere it will have a disastrous effect on communications, which by all accounts are shaky enough already—rumour has it that the proposed change delights the Chinese! And, when a large proportion of the people's democratically elected representatives are no longer able to understand one syllable of their country's language, proceedings in the Lok Sabha will degenerate from the present tragi-comedy to undiluted farce.

I spent a pleasant evening with the Peace Corps boys, catching up on my letters and reports and enjoying a first-class Mozart concert from Russia; in this part of the world the most reliable source of classical music is the U.S.S.R. and on the whole reception is excellent. To-day we were on the road by nine o'clock and despite a strong, persistent head-wind I felt no more than pleasantly tired when we arrived here at 4 p.m., after covering sixty miles; so apparently getting back into training isn't going to be the painful process I'd expected.

At Baijnath, eleven miles from Palampur, the Kangra valley ends and from here the road climbs very steeply for about three miles before crossing the state boundary into Himachal Pradesh. Twelve miles further on comes another stiff climb and then for thirty-five miles one is descending gradually from a 4,000-foot pass to Mandi, which is only 2,400 feet above sea-level. Thus far we have been following the road to Simla, but though I remarked on what lovely country this is when first seeing it last month, I hadn't really appreciated its beauty—one doesn't from a Land-Rover seat!

To-day there was very little traffic, beyond the occasional local bus, and as these rough mountains and stony valleys offer little encouragement to settlers, most of the people we passed to-day were Tibetans walking to Dharamsala to receive His Holiness's blessing and visit their children there. Some were also bringing children for admission to the camp, and I examined fifteen of these Tiblets, twelve of whom appeared to be in the best of health; of the other three one had a very bad cough and may be a T.B. case and two had chronic dysentery and looked quite emaciated.

In Delhi I had been given a letter written in Tibetan explaining the purpose of my Kulu tour—but of course none of these parents could read. However, the mere fact that I produced a document in their own script reconciled them to the peculiar behaviour of the white female cyclist who suddenly dismounted, stripped their children by the wayside and scrutinized them all over!

Roz was being pushed up a steep slope when we encountered the first group of Tibetans; before seeing them I had heard gales of laughter from round a corner of the mountain and known that they were coming—simply because Indians, on the whole, *don't* laugh in the course of their everyday life. What a gay people these refugees are! You get ten smiles from a group of ten Tibetans and one smile (if you're lucky) from a group of ten Indians. Moreover, you can never be quite sure *why* you're getting the one Indian smile, whereas you know you're getting the ten Tibetan smiles out of sheer benevolence towards the world in general.

My inside is still giving a poor welcome to solids so I stopped often at tea-houses to refuel on that heavily sweetened beverage which passes for tea in India. It's a characteristic of Indian villages and small towns that whenever foreigners appear everyone who speaks English collects around as if by magic, and to-day I used these conversational opportunities to test local reactions to Tibetans. It's sad, but inevitable and understandable, that the refugees are extremely unpopular—and the reason usually given for not liking them was their personal filthiness, which to a Hindu of any caste is unforgivable. Nor can one criticize the Indians for taking up this attitude. Their religious scruples about bodily cleanliness obviously originated in the absolute necessity for it in a climate like theirs—and the various infections to which the refugees are so prone prove the Hindu point. Yet most of those to whom I spoke to-day admitted that they found the Tibetans uniquely gentle and honest—though many Indians probably regard the latter virtue as a form of stupidity.

Yesterday I picked up an interesting piece of information. The Tibetan road-workers in the Chumba valley have recently presented a new Willys jeep to His Holiness and this vehicle was bought out of their accumulated savings with cheerful disregard for the fact that His Holiness already possesses a fleet of motors. Undoubtedly the Dalai Lama will convert this gift to the benefit of refugees somewhere, providing the decision is left to himself, but what intrigues me is the financial significance of this presentation. If road-workers can afford to buy a jeep out of their savings then they can certainly afford to contribute substantially to the maintenance of their children.

This town is a most attractive little place, with mountains crouching close on every side and the River Beas frisking along in its deep bed—though all local rivers are rather subdued during these months of frozen snows. The landscape was quite wintry to-day; many trees were leafless, others wore our sort of October colours and the meagre grass was brown. But the sky remained that intense blue which we call 'exaggerated' on postcards and when one got out of the wind the sun was warm. To-night I'm staying at the Dak-bungalow and it's good to sit here writing quietly in my own room, beside an electric fire that doesn't work, with Roz leaning against the end of the bed and both of us feeling younger after the day's run.

TIBETAN ROAD-CAMP NEAR PANDOH: 21 DECEMBER

When we left Mandi at eight o'clock this morning it was very chilly, with a dense river-mist filling the valley. But soon the first rays of the sun penetrated the gorge and the mist suddenly turned to a pinky-gold softness floating over the water—and a few moments later had vanished. Yet for another two hours it remained cold in the shadow of the giant cliffs that rise sheer to more than a thousand feet on both sides of the river.

There is one-way traffic only over the twenty-five miles of this narrow, twisting road through the Mandi-Larji gorge, but at many dangerous bends Tibetans are now blasting away the cliff-face and before long normal traffic should be possible. Actually there was no traffic to-day, one way or the other, though in summer quite a number of tourists come to Kulu.

As we went up the gorge I quoted to myself from *Kubla Khan*, where Coleridge refers to the Beas under its ancient name of Alph.

Where Alph, the sacred river, ran
Through caverns measureless to man
  Down to a sunless sea . . .
And here were forests ancient as the hills,
Enfolding sunny spots of greenery.

But O, that deep romantic chasm which slanted
Down the green hill athwart the cedarn cover!
A savage place! as holy and enchanted
As e'er beneath a waning moon was haunted
By woman wailing for her demon-lover!
And from this chasm, with ceaseless turmoil seething,
As if this earth in fast thick pants were breathing,
A mighty fountain momently was forced. . . .

I little thought, when resentfully swotting these lines more than
twenty years ago, that one day I would travel through this
'cavern measureless to man'. So accurately does Coleridge
describe both the physical aspect and the atmosphere of the
gorge that it is difficult to believe he never saw or felt it; perhaps
opium has stranger side-effects than we know of.

I spent most of the morning finding and examining the forty-
eight Tiblets who live in the road-camp between Mandi and
Pandoh. That camp is situated at river-level, and to approach it
safely from the road one would need the agility of either a goat
or a Tibetan. It's a small settlement of about one hundred
adults, most of whom work all day on the road far above;
however, a few elderly relatives remain among the tents and
prevent the children from getting into too much mischief. This
group owns two milking buffaloes, which like all Indian cattle
appear to live on fresh air. The tents in all these camps are
ex-army models provided by the P.W.D. and some of them are
in bad repair; even the sound ones must seem a very poor
substitute for the yak-hair tents of Tibet, which were proof
against any extremes of temperature and usually wore well for
about fifteen years. Unfortunately such tents are very heavy
and cumbersome, and so few of the refugees succeeded in bringing them to India.

The foreman of this gang is a Sikh who lives in Mandi and

whose directions are translated by the camp-leader, an ex-officer of the Tibetan army. This handsome, rather sad-looking man speaks Hindi quite well but naturally knows no English, so our conversation was confined to basic questions and answers about food and health.

I'm spending the night here at Pandoh camp, which is one of the biggest in the area—one could call it a tent-village, for it accommodates 660 people, including eighty-seven Tiblets. Over 500 adolescents and adults are building a new road along the precipitous mountain on the other side of the Beas. Children under fifteen are not meant to work on the roads, but some of them do; the fifteen- to eighteen-year-olds earn one and six-pence a day. Ninety per cent of Indian road-making is still done by hand, with blasting as the only supplement to human energy, but on this particular section a bull-dozer is in action operated by Indians, which indicates the strategic importance of the new road. It's quite terrifying to stand on the opposite bank of the river—no more than fifty yards wide at this point—and to look up at that gigantic machine edging its way along a narrow shelf newly blasted out of the virgin cliff. Dislodged hunks of mountain come continuously bouncing and rumbling downwards to splash into the Beas and soon I realized that this was forbidden territory; when the foreman noticed me he began to shout in-audibly and to gesticulate in a manner which said plainly enough that I was to go back where I came from. Some ten minutes after my retreat up to the camp there was a terrific ex-plosion, of such force that the ground beneath my feet trembled as in an earthquake. Great jagged fragments of mountain went hurtling through the air in all directions, some landing on this side of the river—which explained the foreman's aversion to my presence there.

Later, when I spoke to this man, he confirmed what his colleague had said to me earlier to-day—that because of their great strength, energy and nimbleness the Tibetans are ideally suited to road-making. Certainly it demands all these qualities; it's awe-inspiring to see half a dozen men and women tie ropes around a colossal rock, push and pull it across the road to the edge of the gorge and leap acrobatically aside as it goes over. Then one of them scampers gaily down the dangerous slope

above the torrent to retrieve the rope, secures it around his waist
and climbs swiftly back to the road. I asked how long it takes
to widen one corner at this rate of progress, but no one cared
to commit themselves to a definite reply. However, though
these labours may sound to us like some form of infernal
punishment the Tibetans seem positively to enjoy them, if one
is to judge by their beaming faces and incessant singing of jolly
choruses; it's beyond me where they get the breath to sing
while performing such feats.

I've now seen for myself a little of the road-camp dangers and
discomforts, from the Tiblets' point of view. Babies are normally
taken from the tents to the road-works on their mothers' backs
and are then transferred to little 'cradles' made of wooden
boxes, while 'Amela' gets on with the job, stopping at the
appropriate intervals to feed her infant. Toddlers also sometimes accompany their parents, if there is no one at home to
care for them, but their obedience to parental orders means that
they are less accident-prone than might be imagined. Yet those
serious illnesses and accidents which do befall both adults and
children are inevitably neglected in the camps—often with fatal
results. The choice lies between separating hundreds of children
from their parents, as a precautionary measure, or leaving the
families united and accepting the consequent disasters as the
lesser of two evils. Unfortunately our cushioned society has
become so obsessed by physical safety that many Westerners
regard removal from the Danger Zone as the only proper solution to the problem—and they tend to push this attitude onto
a people who are traditionally resigned to such hazards.

The leader of Pandoh camp is a dignified, elderly man named
Lobsang Dowa, who speaks only Tibetan; but he has a most
efficient interpreter who is fluent in Hindi and also knows a fair
amount of English. This young man—Pasang—met me on my
arrival, carried Roz up the steep stone 'stairs' to the level
stretch of ground on which the camp is situated and then
brought me on a 'conducted tour'. He told me that these families have now been established here for fourteen months and the
community has its own cobbler, tailor, butcher and vegetable
gardens. It also has a dispensary tent, stocked by the Tom
Dooley Foundation and American Emergency Relief, and until

Road-workers' camp, Kulu
Tibetan road workers moving rocks by hand

Parents bringing children to the nursery
The Kulu Valley

recently, when the Tibetan authorities at Dharamsala quarrelled with the Indian doctor in charge, a Tom Dooley Foundation Mobile Medical Unit toured these camps about once a
fortnight. This service helped to keep the health situation from
deteriorating beyond control, as far as T.B. and injuries were
concerned, yet its limitations were many and the fact that no
other camp has anyone of Pasang's ability to supervise the
carrying out of the doctor's instructions meant that his fort-
nightly visits were often wasted. Pasang has had no medical
training, but has taught himself enough to be able to cope
efficiently with minor diseases and mishaps—and to recognize
those cases which require more specialized treatment.

There are 215 children from this camp in Dharamsala, Dalhousie, Mussoorie and Simla and I see no reason why they
could not have been here at Pandoh for the past fourteen
months. Educational opportunities equal to those available in
the schools could be provided on the spot—and so could improved medical attention. Such a project would perhaps de-
mand more organization on the part of the relief agencies, but
it would certainly require no more money than is being spent
at the moment—possibly less—and it could avert a great deal
of unhappiness.

One feels here that one has got as close to the Tibetan way
of life as is possible; in contrast to this camp Dharamsala seems
cosmopolitan. When the eighty-seven Tiblets who remain had
been examined, and my findings jotted down, I took a stroll
around the 'village', with its 'streets' of beaten earth between
the rows of tents. The men who would be going on night-shift
at 8 p.m. were sitting drinking illegally brewed 'chang' and
playing dice or mahjong—Tibetans love gambling—and it was
touching to see that their stakes were of Tibetan coinage; an act
of faith if ever there was one. Many of the people used the old
greeting-form of rural Tibet, and on my approach bowed low
and stuck out their tongues three times. Everywhere I was
welcomed graciously, if at times shyly, but the comparative
aloofness of the children was very apparent. Unlike their less
fortunate brothers and sisters in the various nurseries, who cling
to any passing stranger in the hopes of receiving some affection,
these Tiblets had shown a normal childish timidity when I first

L

appeared. Yet while being examined outside the Dispensary
tent they were as docile and uncomplaining as any of 'my'
Tiblets at Dharamsala.

To-night lousy sheep-skins have been spread for my benefit
on the smooth earth floor of the Dispensary tent. I had brought
bread and bananas for my supper (this being a prudent anti-
dysentery diet), but Pasang insisted on serving me three eggs
fried in rancid ghee—though eggs are both scarce and very
expensive in this region. It remains to be seen how my inside
will respond to this manifestation of hospitality.

### MANALI: 22 DECEMBER

From Mandi to Pandoh the Beas is on one's left, going towards
Kulu, but at Pandoh there is a break in the gorge and for a
half-mile or so the river curves south, to find a way through the
mountains. On the outskirts of Pandoh village a suspension
bridge takes the road to the north bank and when the gorge
closes in again, the Beas is on one's right for the remaining
twelve miles to Aut.

By eight o'clock this morning we were on our way—after the
proudly beaming Pasang had served me with another three
fried eggs—and we arrived here at six o'clock. Those sixty-eight
miles were all uphill and involved so much walking that to-night
I feel quite exhausted. But what a glorious region this is! Mild
exhaustion is a small price to pay for the joy of seeing Kulu on
a sunny winter's day.

This 'Valley of the Gods'—to give it its alternative and more
appropriate name—begins at Aut, where the Mandi-Larji
gorge ends, and continues for about fifty-five miles. At no point
is it more than a mile wide and at every turn of the road its
beauty increases. The last twenty-five miles from Kulu town to
here are almost as lovely as the Hindu Kush—and almost as
desolate. By this stage one has risen to about 5,000 feet and as
the road climbs the final 1,000 feet to Manali the landscape
becomes really wintry. Many bare oaks and elms and chestnuts
stood out blackly against the evening sky, flocks of rooks and
starlings flew noisily towards their roosts and dry leaves rustled
along the road before the wind. Yet some trees, down the valley,

still glowed in autumn reds and yellows, looking rich and splendid against a dark background of distant pine-forests. On the lower slopes patches of new snow dazzled from clearings between pine-trees, while the white brilliance on sharp, remote summits was almost painful beneath an intense blue sky.

I had hoped to find a Tibetan camp near here, but it's further up, towards the Rothang Pass, so I'm staying at a rest-house where there is no food, water, light or heating. There's only one answer that I know of to this sort of situation and luckily I noticed its source on our way through the bazaar—'Spirit Merchant'! Having purchased some of this gentleman's wares, as a Christmas present to myself, I'm now slightly drunk and very warm, despite six inches of snow outside.

We passed several camps to-day where ragged prayer-flags were flying, and of course I at first assumed them to be Tibetan, but on investigation I discovered that they were the winter settlements of some Spiti nomads. The inhabitants of Lahoul and Spiti are racially, religiously and linguistically akin to the Tibetans, though their remote valleys and plateaux are now politically part of India. The only way for an outsider to distinguish between Tibetans and Spitis is by studying the women's aprons; Tibetan aprons have horizontal stripes, Spiti aprons have perpendicular stripes. Similarly, when pilgrims from Ladakh came to Dharamsala to receive His Holiness's blessing we could distinguish them from the Tibetans only by noting that their women wore aprons both front and back.

In Spiti as in Tibet, the yak is the most important item of livestock and these nomads bring a supply of dzo butter with them on their annual migration—so it was while being entertained in one of these camps this afternoon that I first sampled the genuine Tibetan buttered tea and tsampa. Contrary to popular opinion this is not a revolting mess but a palatable and sustaining meal. But I took four sulphaguanidine as a second course, because of my present delicate condition—which has not been improved by that surfeit of fried eggs.

On my way through the bazaar to patronize the Spirit Merchant I called briefly at the local Mission Hospital where Dr Snell, his wife and two nurses—one of them an Irishwoman—do what they can to care for the local Tibetan workers. Dr Snell remarked on the Tibetan susceptibility to T.B. at these altitudes and gave it as his opinion that though the roadworkers in general now show such cheerful energy it can only be a matter of time before the combination of heavy labour and protein deficiency breaks their natural stamina. When one remembers the amount of protein consumed in Tibet this seems only too likely.

TIBETAN ROAD-CAMP NEAR FOOT OF ROTHANG PASS:
23 DECEMBER

The road-surface from Mandi to Kulu town is excellent and from Kulu to Manali it remains tolerable, but Dr Snell informed me yesterday that no road—only a rough bridle-path —exists between Manali and the tiny hamlet of Rahola at the foot of the Rothang Pass. So as the distance is only ten miles I decided to walk, leaving Roz at the rest-house, where the decrepit but amiable chowkidar swore to guard her with his life. Actually this path, though rough and stony, is no worse than many of the main roads Roz endured on our way through Persia and Afghanistan—and it's a lot better than some! Yet I was glad I hadn't risked taking her to-day since our spare-tyre situation is precarious at the moment.

When I left Manali at ten o'clock this morning last night's snow had almost vanished, but it was cool enough for me to need a sweater. From the rest-house the bridle-path descends through a wood of giant pines, crosses the narrow young Beas by a cantilever bridge and turns left up the north bank of the river.

Yesterday's trek was superb, but to-day's had a unique quality—not only because of its beauty, but because for hours on end I was surrounded by that strangely moving stillness which pervades unpeopled mountains with the force of a living spirit.

In these regions the landscape changes its aspect dramatically. Between Manali and Rahola one is in a different world from that of the lower Kulu valley—a world of broad, vivid green moors, bounded by the silver-grey rockiness of its mountain walls, their white crests encircling the horizon. On some of the precipices isolated pines grow from what appears to be bare rock, and this phenomenon occurs right up to the 10,000-foot summits of the lower peaks. The effect is extraordinarily beautiful, as these simple lines of rock and tree sweep upwards in harmony. All day the sky remained quite clear but the few wisps of white cloud that did go drifting over the highest peaks looked dingy beside those immaculate snow-caps. It was very unpoetic of me, but I couldn't help thinking of 'Persil Washes Whiter!' Even up here at the head of the valley it got so hot around mid-day that I had to remove my sweater and walk in shirt-sleeves; but now, at 7 p.m., the frost is severe.

There are only twenty-three Tiblets in this small camp, which is sheltered by a straggling copse of pines on the river-bank. Next week these workers will be packing up and moving down to the Kangra valley until the worst of the winter is over.

The camp-leader's tent, in which I'm receiving hospitality, accommodates a family of eight—granny, her two sons, their wives and two babies of seven and four months. Granny and I are to share sheep-skins tonight so it's likely that by morning my already considerable stock of vermin will have acquired companions. Happily lice and bugs don't discommode me to any great extent, but dearly as I love the Tibetans it is impossible to get accustomed to the nauseating odour of that rancid butter with which they lavishly oil their hair and anoint their bodies. When used on the hair this repulsive unguent is alleged to deter lice and when applied to the body it keeps out the cold; yet however practical its uses may be no one save a Tibetan could ever become resigned to its stink. I'm sitting beside a wood-fire now, writing by flame-light with wood-smoke tears streaming down my face—but at least this acrid smoke does something to obliterate the butter stench. Even the babies' almost bald heads have been plastered with the ghastly stuff. In all these camps Tiblets' heads are similarly treated and, having had scores of them laid on my bosom within the past few days, my shirt is now so saturated with grease that even when walking through the wide open spaces I cannot get away from the stink.

It's interesting to observe that the unexpected arrival of a foreign guest does not throw Tibetans into the state of embarrassed confusion common among Indian peasants in similar circumstances. This may be partly explained by the fact that Tibetan peasants have no conception of standards other than their own, whereas Indians are uncomfortably aware of the style to which Westerners are accustomed. But one suspects that it is also connected with the Tibetan temperament and with their freedom from religio-social taboos; these people display a splendid mixture of ease and formality while receiving you into a simple tent and before many moments have passed they manage to make you feel completely at home. There is no English speaker in this camp, but the language barrier has long since gone crashing and we're all the best of friends on a system of smiles and gestures.

As usual I brought my own food with me to-day but—again as usual—I'm not to be allowed to touch it. A form of porridge is now being cooked for supper and into this Granny has just thrown handfuls of chopped onions and dates, while I looked on with the resignation of despair. By all natural laws the diet of the past few days should have completed my internal disintegration, but instead I seem to be rapidly returning to normal.

TIBETAN ROAD-CAMP NEAR RAISON: 24 DECEMBER

Christmas Eve in the Workhouse—scene as before—rancid butter and wood-smoke and eccentric porridge for supper. Fortunately I bought myself another Christmas present on the way back through Manali, which was a horribly extravagant thing to do—yet perhaps such extravagance is forgivable when there's no one else around to give me a present. Indian whisky is about the same price as Irish whisky, but that's the only point of resemblance between the two distillations. My plastic mug is showing signs of *melting* in a very odd way since it began to come into nightly contact with Indian whisky—which may account for the brew's curiously chemical flavour.

I left Granny and Company at half-past eight this morning and by walking briskly was back with Roz at eleven o'clock. Then we enjoyed the twenty-five mile freewheel back to Kulu town, before branching off for an eight-mile trek to this camp. There are fifty-eight Tiblets here, the majority in excellent health.

To-day several men passed us carrying water in bear-skins. I've seen pig-skins used thus in Spain and goat-skins in many places but bear-skins were a novelty to me—and those bears were so massive that it takes two men to carry a full skin. I just hope never to meet such a skin containing its original owner!

What a splendid Christmas Eve this is—truly a silent night, and a holy one, in the shadow of these mountains.

# 10

## *The Valley of Refuge*

What a Christmas Day! If I live to be a hundred I am unlikely ever to 'celebrate' the festival more strangely. Really I'm in no condition to-night for diary-writing, but it's best to get it all down while the details are fresh in my mind.

When we left Raison at 7.30 a.m. the sun was just up, but not yet over the mountains, and the bitterly cold air numbed me as I freewheeled down the valley. By 8.30 we had reached Bhuntar, six miles from Kulu town, and here I chanced to notice a weather-beaten little sign-post pointing off the main road and saying—'Jari: 14 ms.' On seeing this name I remembered that Jari was the next village to Malana—a unique settlement which I had supposed to be nearer Spiti and inaccessible during winter. I was then making for a Tibetan camp some twenty miles away, but when I realized that Malana lay so near the temptation to explore was too much for me. I said to myself, 'Dash it, this is Christmas, why not take a short vacation?' So I left the main road, crossed the Beas by suspension bridge and headed up the Parvati valley.

Malana is an autonomous community of some 600 people, who live on a 9,000-foot plateau, independent of all outside influences, and one of the many remarkable things about them is their language. Some philologists claim to find definite links between Malani, Magyar and Finnish; it is also allied—more understandably—to Pharsi. Archaeologists and anthropologists estimate that the Malanis have been living on this remote plateau for about 5,000 years, and their religion, a primitive form of Hinduism, consists in the worship of the god Jamdagnishri—also known, more pronounceably, as Jamlu. Jamlu is believed to be a sort of demon-spirit and, like the Malanis, he has an independent nature and does not pay homage even to

Raghunathjee, the principal god of the Kulu valley, to whom most other local gods do reverence. All the cultivated lands around Malana are regarded as Jamlu's property, the Malanis being merely his tenants. The village treasure is also his property, and the treasure-house is rumoured to contain uncountable quantities of cash, jewels, gold and silver ornaments and the silver images of a horse which are the customary offering to this particular god.

To the Malanis their territory is known as the 'Valley of Refuge' and unsubstantiated oral tradition says that the original inhabitants fled there during some long-forgotten crisis. Now, out of gratitude to Jamlu, who protected their ancestors, these people unquestioningly offer refuge to anyone fleeing from any sort of trouble—though only caste Hindus are permitted to enter the village itself. This provision of sanctuary is occasionally of use to local criminals, who know that the villagers won't hand them over to the police.

The Malanis have never had anything to do with any ruling power and they take no part in the life of the nation. A committee of eleven elders governs the community, and when the Government of India insisted on opening a village school twelve years ago the elders forbade anyone to attend it—though for the past five years it has had one pupil. When anyone falls ill they are taken to the chief, who asks them what moral wrong they have done to cause the illness (5,000-year-old psychology!) and gives them a magic brew of herbs. If they die despite this brew the wrong done is presumed to have been too heinous for reparation in this life and they are then cremated after the orthodox Hindu fashion, on the banks of the little Malana nullah. On the death of the head of a household his goods are divided equally between all his children, who are expected to contribute a share each to keep their mother in the state to which she was accustomed. Marriages are arranged on the usual Hindu basis, but divorces may be had simply by paying Rs. 20 (about £1 10s.) to the wife—an unusual deviation, since throughout India proper they are very difficult to obtain. Theft is unknown in this community and any crime is rare, but if there is a question of one of two people being guilty both parties bring a lamb to the chief, who slits the animals' throats and inserts an identical quantity of cyanide into each slit—and the owner of the lamb which dies first is regarded as the guilty party.

The Malanis collect the roots of a plant used to make incense, and many medicinal herbs which they sell or barter, but most of their cash comes from hunting the musk-deer. This animal abounds here—though being very fast and elusive it is extremely difficult to shoot. I was told to-day that one musk is worth Rs. 1,000 (£75) and that so far this season the Malanis have shot thirty-five male deer. These figures sound almost incredible; if they are true then the Malanis' austere mode of life is from choice, not necessity! Or does most of this cash have to go into Jamlu's treasure-house?

The fourteen miles from Bhuntar to Jari were all uphill, through yet another indescribably lovely valley—and it was yet another perfect day of clear, deep blue skies and warm, golden sunshine, with the air so pure that merely to breathe was a joy. It's not surprising that the Kulu valley and its side valleys were chosen by sages and saints in Vedic times for meditation and prayer—I'd choose them too, if I were given to either meditation or prayer! And Mr Nehru, a regular visitor to Manali to get away from it all, is evidently in agreement with me.* Each of these valleys, and each hamlet in each valley, has its own tutelary deity, and as the region has been virtually untouched by modern developments of Hinduism the local religion remains strongly tinged with animism. Throughout all India's history the Kulu valley (known as Kiu-Lu-To in the days when it was at the southern boundary of Kubla Khan's Empire) was never conquered or occupied till the British came; in recent times the area was called the State of Rupi and had its own rajah (usually a pretty degenerate type) until the line faded out in the 1920s.

The road we travelled from Bhuntar was part of one of the old trade-routes going from India through Spiti and Tibet to China. It's no more than a track and has the worst surface we've met since leaving Gilgit, with the difference that if you went over the edge here you'd only fall 500 feet, instead of 1,500 as in the Indus Gorge. The Indian Government is now

* He stayed at Manali during the week before his death in May, 1964.

investigating local uranium deposits but so far has not determined their value—or isn't telling if it has! Large notices, warning All Unauthorized Persons to keep off the relevant sites,
come as a shock when they suddenly appear in this otherwise
unspoiled region. For two miles this morning, about half-way
to Jari, the cliffs on my right were gigantic walls of rough,
red marble and the track was strewn with red chips and dust,
producing a fantastic effect in the brilliant sunshine; I walked
through a dream-like rosy haze and even the emerald river,
flashing along the valley floor far below, appeared to have
changed colour. Between Bhuntar and Jari we passed two tiny
hamlets, where the people were as grim and dour as elsewhere
in Kulu: I don't ever remember travelling among such unfriendly peasants as these. Yet when you stop for tea, or to buy
fruit or cigarettes, they are courteous—it's just that they give
the general impression of *not* wanting strangers around the
place. Aloofness is quite against my principles as a traveller but
I've abandoned the habit of saluting passers-by, since the
response is always a cold stare.

At 11 a.m. we reached Jari, which was just what I had
expected it to be—an impoverished huddle of disintegrating
mud and wood hovels where milk was scarce and fruit, eggs
and sugar were unobtainable, but where the surrounding
beauty was so exhilarating that to a non-resident nothing else
mattered. Going straight to the Forest Rest House I received
the chowkidar's permission to leave Roz there for the night and
then asked him to show me where the path to Malana began.
The poor man obviously thought me off my head (now I know
why!) and said 'Malana *ne*! You go *Manikand*—yes?' (Manikand is famous for its hot springs and is approached from Jari
by a seven-mile bridle-path.) I was shaking my head and firmly
repeating 'Malana—I go *Malana*,' when such a fantastic coincidence occurred that I can only regard it as a Christmas present
from Jari's tutelary deity.

Two constables of the Punjab Armed Police suddenly materi-
alized beside me to enquire into my presence in a Restricted
Zone, and having sorted that one out I enquired into *their* presence, since tiny hamlets don't normally have resident police-
men. In reply they explained that they were about to conduct

an election agent to Malana, as the three-yearly Punjabi state elections are now in progress. At that point we were joined by the election agent, a plainsman from Chandigarh who was shivering despite layers of woollen garments and what felt to me like hot sun. His present duties were evidently not suiting him in any way and he wore a distinctly martyred expression— which temporarily changed to one of astonishment when he saw me talking to his bodyguard. On discovering my destination he looked rather startled and said, 'But *why* are you going there?' I answered, 'Because I want to,' which seemed to me a flawless reason; yet it obviously struck my companion as hopelessly inadequate, if not actually insane. The agent then pointed out, in words of one syllable, that people only went to Malana under compulsion. 'The Malanis are dirty savages,' he concluded, 'and the way is very tedious.' I discounted both these statements, realizing that by Hindu standards I too was a dirty savage, not having washed for a week. In reply to my query as to why a Punjabi election agent had to visit this autonomous community I was told that the Malanis are now citizens of Asia's biggest democracy and have to be given the opportunity to vote. I next asked what happens when the election party reaches the village and the agent said that they put up a notice (which no one can read), improvise a polling booth (which is pointedly ignored by the villagers) and then spend two nights and one day gambling mildly together before returning to Jari! We were now joined by a friend of the agent, who was accompanying the party to make a four at cards and dice; to me the whole thing was enchantingly Gilbertian and I happily received their reluctant consent to my accompanying the expedition.

One of the most pleasing features of life here is that for a trek like this people simply stand up and go, minus the tiresome paraphernalia of picnic-baskets, cameras, binoculars, night-clothes, first-aid kits, etc., with which Westerners would fussily encumber themselves in similar circumstances. But there was one important preparation to be made for this particular expedition. It is a grievous offence against the Malanis' religion to bring leather into their territory, so we had to remove all leather objects from our persons. The police took off their belts and replaced their rifle-straps with ropes, the agent's friend grumpily exchanged his leather fur-lined cap for a woollen balaclava and the agent himself almost tearfully abandoned his long leather gauntlets. My boots were of rubber and canvas so when I had pronouned myself 'clean' we set off.

From Jari the path descended to river-level, through dark pine-forests where unmelted snow made the steep path treacherous to our rubber boots. Then we crossed the wide, rapid nullah by a nonchalant bridge of frost-slippery planks and were again in sunshine, at the point where the Parvati nullah is joined by the more turbulent Malana nullah, which we were now going to follow up its narrow ravine.

This stage—a gradual five-mile climb—provided such a remarkable concentration of hazards that the business of avoiding death occupied 90% of my attention and the beauties of the ravine impressed me only during our rest halts. The agent, on his third visit to Malana, was our leader—if so decisive a title may be bestowed on a man who viewed the whole performance with frank horror. As we struggled upwards I admitted to myself that the Jari chowkidar had been right. Guidance was indeed necessary for this track—to prove the human animal capable of following it rather than to show the way, which in most places could be lost only by falling into the nullah or scaling a 2,000-foot cliff. Among the more stimulating diversions was a cow-hair rope hand-bridge which made me feel like a trapeze artiste without the net, as the torrent thundered hungrily down its bed of boulders beneath my dangling feet. After this came a brief respite—some hundred yards of firm silver sand on which we walked five abreast beside a shallow, more subdued nullah, where the clear green water was like a liquid jewel.

Here one could relax and appreciate the vividly coloured, densely forested slopes of the ravine, where the rest of the party nervously imagined leopards and bears lurking behind every second tree. But this carefree phase did not last long. Soon we had climbed again and were edging our way along a path hardly eighteen inches wide: in places it had crumbled away completely and been casually replaced by a few branches. The nullah was now 300 feet below us, and from this path looked very easy of access by accident. After about half a mile we descended again to find another test of acrobatic skill; a giant pine trunk had been laid against the cliff where the path ended, to serve as a ladder down to river-level. The 'steps' once hacked in the wood had long since been worn away and, as this part of the ravine is permanently shadowed, the whole trunk was covered in ice. To us it seemed a suicidal contraption; looking down I wondered whether my imminent death would come from a broken neck on the rocks or through drowning in the nullah. Then I went over gallantly, following the agent and hoping for drowning. But of course instinct took charge where intelligence had failed and I found myself sensibly sliding down the trunk, with arms and legs wrapped firmly around it, so that within seconds I was comparatively safe on a vast slab of rock that sloped steeply towards the water. The police followed, their complexions perceptibly ashen, and on landing beside me the elder one promptly vomited in reaction. I hadn't gone to quite this extreme myself but I couldn't have agreed more!

For the next quarter of an hour we had to leap goat-like from rock to rock in the midst of the swirling nullah—yet this seemed a mere parlour game after the tree-trunk ordeal. Then we came up against a gloriously foaming waterfall and stopped to rest beneath a cliff so high and so precipitous that its top was invisible. At this stage it was not clear to me where we went from here; the alternatives seemed to be a struggle through fifty feet of crashing water or a climb up this monstrous mountain, which had obviously been designed for the exclusive use of monkeys.

After thirty minutes' rest the agent rose to his feet and said succinctly—'Here we go up.' And so we did. We went up every yard of that sheer, 3,000-foot precipice—on which the Malanis have carved a stairway in the rock—and before we had got half-way the ache of my legs and lungs was torture; I almost wept with relief when we came to a ledge where there was space for all of us to collapse speechlessly for another rest. By now my clothes were saturated with sweat and I avidly ate the snow which lay within reach and rubbed its delicious hard coldness on my face and neck—to the wonder of my companions, who were still feeling chilly. Soon we set off again, pulling ourselves up and up and up. Then we saw our first Malanis—three young women, carrying loads as big as themselves, who effortlessly overtook us and disappeared ahead. Their swift agility made me feel like something left out too long in the rain, as I fought for the breath and the energy to drag one foot in front of the other. (I realize that the descent to-morrow, when I intend to return to Jari, will be even more difficult, as it will involve constantly looking down at that unspeakable drop into the nullah.) At 4.15 p.m. we finally crawled over the edge of a little plateau astride the mountain-top and threw ourselves full length on the close-cropped grass.

Lying there, I remembered the tradition which says that the original Malanis fled to this spot from some unspecified enemy whom they reckoned would not pursue them to such a hide-out. And I decided that this tradition is historically sound, since no enemy could possibly harbour enough enmity to penetrate to Malana. I also reflected on the pleasing certainty that here were a place and a people who in A.D. 2063 would be recognizable to my ghost. The most ingenious engineer will never construct as much as a mule-track to Malana, which in fact is not a conventional valley, but a circle of fearsomely steep mountains, on whose upper slopes the Malanis live in unnatural defiance of the laws of gravity.

Having recovered my breath I rose, looked around me and realized that to stand here was an experience worth all the perils and exertions of the trek. To the south stretched the ravine through which we had come, with Jari framed in its narrow opening against a background of distant snow-peaks, now briefly fired by the setting sun. To east and west, close by our 9,000-foot mountain, twins of about 11,000 feet were densely wooded to their rounded summits and on the upper slopes of each a few steady blue columns of smoke marked the spots where deer-hunters were camping for the night. And then, to the north, there was the profound, shadowed Valley of Refuge. Its semi-circular guard of 17,000-foot peaks, all shining in new snow against the blue-green sky, rose austerely from the smooth, wide loveliness of their glaciers—what a sight!

Now the temperature had dropped so sharply that I was shivering all over in my sweat-soaked clothes. The village of Malana was still invisible behind a forest of towering pines—

it became dark as night when we walked through them—and
everywhere on this northern side of the mountain snow lay at
least a foot deep. By 5 p.m. we had reached the outskirts of the
village, having crossed a tricky little glacier, and I saw a collection of some 150 houses straggling up and down the slope. The
majority are two- or three-storey dwellings, securely built of
colossal stone slabs and great tree-trunks, and the combination
of these elemental, unsubdued materials with a distinctive,
compact design creates a curiously stark beauty. But it was the
wooden balconies outside the first-floor rooms which really
astonished me. The sureness and sensitivity of their carvings—
as fine as anything Germany produced in the Golden Age of
Reimenschneider—seems in this superficially uncouth and completely isolated community almost as puzzling as the language.
And the physical appearance of the people increases the mystery, for they look like any other local peasants, though in-
breeding has obviously dulled their intelligence.

I had known that as a non-Hindu I would be 'untouchable'
to the Malanis (a very salutary experience for a European!),
but I had not realized that this means being confined to the
untouchables' path, which skirts the 'caste' houses and of course
the temple. However, Malana is so tiny that even from this path
I could examine most of the buildings and observe that outwardly Jamlu's treasure-house looks much the same as the
family dwellings and is quite unlike the crudely elaborate
temples seen in most Hindu villages. Yet in one respect it is
quite unique: the only entrance to this tall, doorless building
is through a hole in the roof. When the Malanis require money
for any communal expense the *gur*—as they call their priest—
climbs onto the roof, descends into the pitch-dark chamber
and emerges with an armful of whatever comes to hand.
Obviously the value of the treasure thus collected varies from
visit to visit and the Malanis believe that Jamlu wishes them to
spend no more on any particular project than the *gur* chances
to find in his blind gropings.

Unlike the average Hindu god Jamlu is not represented by
any image or idol, but by a slab of stone which lies in the centre
of a small grassy plot at the edge of the village. This stone,
measuring approximately three feet by two across and eighteen

inches high, looks so exactly like millions of other slabs scattered around the region that if I hadn't known about it I would never have guessed its significance. On it animals are sacrificed to Jamlu in the course of religious ceremonies and no one but the *gur* is allowed to touch it. (Some people morbidly maintain that not only animals are sacrificed; certainly the population of Malana has been very successfully kept at six or seven hundred for thousands of years, though migration is unknown among these people. And the cultivatable land around the village could support no more than this number.)

It was nearly dark when my untouchable host came to guide me to his home on the far side of the village. Few people were visible as we skirted Malana, and of those few the women and children registered terror at my appearance and fled from sight, while the men, draped in splendidly coloured home-spun blankets, stood and stared unsmilingly. However, the good-humour and kindness of my host and his family are more than compensating for the general lack of cordiality.

This household consists of a young couple and their two children—a nine-year-old daughter and a two-year-old son. The girl is Malana School's sole pupil, which seems logical enough; as untouchables these people have nothing to lose and possibly something to gain by disobeying the chief's orders and allowing their children to receive some education. (Though when I met the teacher—a pleasant but inconceivably moronic youth from Kulu town—I realized that the child would be better occupied herding flocks instead of attending his lessons.) My hostess is one of the most beautiful women I've ever seen, both in features and expression, and as I watched her from my side of the fire—her face glowing against the darkness beyond —I was irresistibly reminded of the brave, sad innocence of Rembrandt's 'Titus'. Her husband is also exceptionally handsome, and both children have inherited their parents' good looks.

Most Malani houses are stables and granaries as well as dwellings, and hay is stored on the side-balconies, where it protects the living-rooms from the bitter winds. But the untouchables' house is merely a one-roomed cottage, for they have neither live-stock nor grain. Their only possessions are two

M

battered brass cooking-pots, an earthenware mug, an axe, a bedding-roll and the garments they stand up in; this empty room makes a Tibetan tent look over-furnished. A stone fireplace about four feet in circumference lies in the middle of the mud floor, where an unintentional Yule-log some three yards long—the most spectacular I'm ever likely to enjoy!—is now burning merrily with the aid of handfuls of twigs. There is a twelve-inch opening, between the roof of stone slabs and the wall, through which the smoke escapes—and through which icy currents of air from the glaciers sweep in on the assembled company. Everyone squats around the fire while talking, cooking and eating. (Or, in the present case, writing. I'm three-quarters blind after these hours of writing by flickering firelight.)

A magnificent Himalayan sheep-dog—now asleep with his head on my outstretched legs—should really have been listed as a member of the family. He's the size of a small donkey, with a glossy, short-haired black coat, rather blunt nose, white chest and tan-coloured legs—a typical specimen, but even more affectionate than most of his breed. When he first appeared, soon after my arrival, I automatically made encouraging noises and before I knew what had hit me I'd been knocked flat on my back by this vast bundle of lovingness. Having romped ecstatically over me for at least ten minutes His Nibs then ate his supper of boiled potatoes and settled down to sleep. Most Indians treat dogs so abominably that it has done me good to find a normal human-canine relationship operating here.

Our supper consisted of chapattis, and potatoes sliced and simmered in ghee. There were plenty of the latter so I'm not complaining about my Christmas dinner—what more could a good Irishwoman ask than platefuls of Murphies! The Malanis do not normally use tea, sugar or any other non-local product —for very obvious reasons.

A slight crisis occurred while supper was being prepared. As my hostess was making the chapattis her husband began to peel potatoes clumsily with his axe (!), because the household possesses no knife, and after watching this process for a few moments I could stand the sight no longer—partly for the poor man's sake and partly for my own, since I had eaten nothing all day. So I produced my own knife, having drawn it from its leather sheath. Suddenly everyone was motionless and in the tense little silence that followed I became guiltily aware of my *faux pas.* Fortunately I knew enough about Malani customs to react correctly; making the appropriate gestures of remorse I at once produced Rs. 10—the price of the lamb which must be sacrificed to-morrow to placate the insulted Jamlu. And though cynics may here accuse me of being too naïve, no one who had once sensed the Malani atmosphere could doubt the use to which those rupees will be put: this family couldn't possibly consider going happily on with the daily round until their god has been propitiated for such an outrage on his territory.

After supper we had another slight crisis, when the election agent nobly tore himself away from his gambling to ensure that I was comfortable for the night. Admittedly the question of bedding did pose a minor problem; the family has none to spare and any blankets lent me from a 'caste' house would be so contaminated by my body that their owners could never use them again. Yet the solution seemed simple to me—a heap of hay in the corner—and the real complication was caused by my host's indignation at the idea of his guest being bedded down like an animal. However, he was at last induced to agree to this scheme by my emphatic assurances that *all* Irish people habitually sleep in hay.

I've just been out for an essential short stroll before retiring and in the brilliant moonlight this soundless, snow-bright valley seems quite unearthly. I'm not psychic, yet for me Malana has, unexpectedly, a Presence—which is perhaps the natural result of its inhabitants' 5,000-year-old belief that here dwells Jamdagnishri. Undeniably it is an eerie place, lying cold and still and secretive in its high isolation and sending curious intruders away no wiser than when they came.

# 11

## *Over the Jalori Pass*

It's unlike me to sleep badly, especially after a strenuous day; yet last night I woke up repeatedly, feeling alert and uneasy for no apparent reason. There really *is* something uncanny about Malana. I'm usually at my happiest in the most primitive places, but this morning I was quite glad to leave that village— in spite of the beauty of its surroundings and the friendliness of my host and his family.

Admittedly the mice—seemingly millions of them—contributed to my wakefulness, and eventually I composed a fatuous lullaby based on the assumption that my Tibetan-lousy head was attracting the creatures—

> It's nice
> To have lice
> Bringing mice/And rice
> (with spice),
> And dice
> And ice
> At any price.

And finally I went to sleep with one persistent mouse firmly roosting above my left ear.

I was up at 7 a.m. for a breakfast of hot water, chapattis and sliced potatoes fried in ghee. The election party went into a flat spin on hearing that I intended returning to Jari alone, but I ignored their unconvincing arguments about the dangers of meeting leopards, bears (who presumably are all hibernating by now) and other unspecified menaces. The more I see of Indians the more astounded I am by their physical cowardice. Each of these four men said that they wouldn't on any account do such a trek alone, yet the average European woman (not to say man) would think nothing of it once she knew the trail and how best to circumvent its hazards.

It was still very cold when I set off at 8 a.m. and as expected the descent to the nullah was much more nerve-wracking than the ascent had been—though obviously much less exhausting. It took me an hour to reach the foot of that precipice, but then I relaxed and enjoyed every moment of the journey back—even shinning up the pine-trunk 'stairs', with the aid of my knife stuck hilt-deep in the rotten wood, and crossing the rope hand-bridge.

To-day I came across a lot more wild-life than yesterday. I saw:

(1) The monal, a very rare type of pheasant, commonly found only in this valley. A cock flew close by and alighted beneath a tree some four yards away while I was sitting by the river. Its shining dark-green plumage really was quite breath-taking—though in build it didn't look at all pheasant-like to me.

(2) A musk-deer—small as a goat—appeared briefly on the opposite bank of the nullah, scented me and vanished into a tangle of scrub. (My nostrils often caught the whiff of musk, but this was the only one I saw.)

(3) A goral—which is another deer, almost as big as a Jersey cow, with a thick, dark-brown coat. This lovely creature crossed the trail so near that I could almost have touched it, then sighted me and bounded away through the trees.

(4) A couple of flying foxes frisking on the opposite bank: they really are the most enchanting little creatures imaginable and I spent fifteen minutes watching their antics and observing what a highly developed sense of humour they reveal as they play together. With their silky chestnut coats gleaming in the sun they looked at times like two little flames darting through the undergrowth.

(5) A troop of graceful, slender monkeys with very beautiful silver bodies, black heads and tails and enormous liquid eyes; I would have identified them as lemurs if that species were not nocturnal. Perhaps some domestic crisis was keeping them up all day.

(6) An otter, tracked by following its wet tail-marks on flat slabs of rock by the river. Eventually I came on it lunching off

trout and I felt rather bad about interrupting the meal: naturally it took fright on seeing me and slid into a deep pool beneath
an overhanging boulder.

(7) Last and greatest thrill of all—a real live panther,
rippling sinuously up a bare, sheer precipice like a poem of
motion. That indeed was beauty in action.

Needless to say all this nature-study wasn't achieved without
hours of sitting around, and I didn't arrive at the Forest Rest
House until 5.30, by which time it would have been quite dark
but for the moon, whose brilliance here in India never ceases
to astonish and delight me.

After Malana this hut, complete with table, chair and charpoy, is comparatively luxurious—yet I'm thinking enviously of
that yule-log, for no heating is available and by now my fingers
are almost too numb to hold the pen. I'm writing by the light
of a wick floating in a bowl of malodorous mutton-fat and I've
just dined off two flimsy chapattis and a tiny mug of dal. This
fare didn't begin to match my appetite, but one is reluctant to
ask for more when it's quite likely that one has already eaten
the chowkidar's supper.

I forgot to mention a little experiment which I conducted
this morning on the outskirts of Malana. The Malanis prize
cigarettes very highly, as their normal smoke is a hookah filled
only with wood-embers, so when I met two young men collecting firing in the pine-forest I stopped and offered them a
cigarette each, holding out the open packet as one does. They
hesitated for a moment and glanced at each other, before sign-
ing to me to put the packet on the ground. When I had done so
first one and then the other bent down and gingerly removed a
cigarette, taking great care not to touch the packet itself, which
had been vilely polluted by contact with an 'untouchable' hand.
Having pocketed their spoils they grinned a trifle sheepishly and
then withdrew at speed from my unwholesome company.

Now I think a long and, I hope, mouse-free sleep is indicated.

TIBETAN ROAD-CAMP NEAR SHAT: 27 DECEMBER

(I can't refrain from pointing out what a superbly appropriate name this is for a Tibetan camp site!)

To-day has been relatively uneventful, though most enjoyable. We left Jari at 8.30 a.m. and had a bone and screw-shaking freewheel down to the main road at Bhuntar. In fact I walked about five of the fourteen miles, both to spare Roz's tyres and to give myself another opportunity to admire this valley.

Breakfast at Jari had consisted of one chapatti and a cup of ersatz tea, so I stopped at a Bhuntar eating-house to devour a four-egg omelette—my first sustaining meal for many days. The people of this locality are the poorest I've yet seen in India, though Kulu is famous for its fruit, particularly apples. One suspects that hitherto the orchards have been the monopoly of a few rich men and that the peasants have been too ignorant to make the best of their land. Now, however, the Government is subsidizing and supervising the planting of small orchards, and is actively encouraging poultry-farming. One sees few goats or sheep, the pasturage being too poor. Cows are also scarce, and half a pound is their average daily yield.

On leaving Bhuntar we freewheeled smoothly down the main road for about eighteen miles—and then turned up another side valley to find this camp of 263 adults and forty-four children. The little tent village was established here a year ago and will remain *in situ* for at least another three months, so again there is no real obstacle to it being a home for most of the workers' children.

In each of these camps I met the parents of some of my favourites at Dharamsala. Usually, on hearing that I've come from there, they introduce themselves with anxious enquiries about their children, but occasionally I recognize them by some marked family resemblance or because they've been to visit the Nursery recently.

So far, in the course of my Tiblet-checking in all these road-camps, I've found nine ex-Dharamsala victims who spent periods of varying lengths at the Nursery before being removed because their parents were shocked by the deterioration in their health. Nine is a small number, yet it cheers me to know that there is a hard core of strong-minded Tibetans among the road-workers.

TIBETAN ROAD-CAMP NEAR LUHRI: 28 AND 29 DECEMBER

There was no time for diary-writing last night, as will soon become apparent.

We left Shat at 7 a.m. yesterday and had covered the twenty-four miles to Shoja by mid-day. This camp is at 8,800 feet and over the last sixteen miles the rough track climbs steeply towards the foot of the Jalori Pass. For the first time since we left Dharamsala the sky was cloudy and the sides of this long, narrow valley were flecked with snow. There was more cultivation here than elsewhere in Kulu and the ingenious terracing reminded me of the Murree area of Pakistan. Clumps of pine-trees looked black beside gleaming snow-drifts, and far above the track wooden farm-houses were adhering—somehow—to apparently sheer cliff-faces at altitudes of more than 10,000 feet. Beneath that dark grey sky this seemed a sombre, slightly awesome valley.

Shoja camp is a big settlement of 180 tents, the majority in good condition and each with its pile of firewood stacked beside it; luckily there is no shortage of fuel in this heavily forested region. These tents shelter 400 adults (approximately) and 161 children (precisely). I spent four hours examining the Tiblets and found that 118 appeared to be in perfect health—against all the odds, for they rarely get milk or meat and live mainly on rice and dal. The chief complaints of the other forty-three were dysentery, otitis media, gingivitis and what I suspect to be worms and T.B. The camp has been established here for the past year and will be at least another year on the same site; a brand new road is being built over the difficult Jalori Pass and work hasn't yet progressed very far. As I was being given these facts by the young English-speaking interpreter anger filled me; considering the numbers of wealthy relief agencies operating in Tibland it is outrageous that no worthwhile medical aid has been provided for such a camp. This neglect can only be explained by criminal stupidity on someone's part.

I had intended spending the night with the Tibetans, as usual, and crossing the Jalori Pass to-day en route for the next camp at Luhri; but the interpreter and the camp-leader both advised me to cross the pass that evening, as blizzards were expected in the area to-day. They said that Khanag, the first rest house on the other side, was only ten miles away, and generally implied that this was an easy trek which could be done in about four hours. At this stage my reasoning faculty apparently broke down and I unquestioningly accepted their advice, overlooking two elementary facts—(*a*) that a mountain-pass graded as 'easy' by Tibetans might be far from easy to a European and (*b*) that having already that day pushed Roz up to 8,800 feet I wasn't really in a fit state to continue to 10,700 feet. Yet I then felt quite fresh, after my four hours of sitting examining Tiblets, so at 4.30 p.m. we blithely set out for Khanag.

The first three miles were less steep than the previous sixteen and I cycled them slowly—but then the trouble started. On this bridle-path over the pass (which is officially open only from May to September) the gradients are utterly inhuman; further-more, where the Tibetans have been widening the track by hacking away the earthy cliff on one side, we suddenly found ourselves slithering in ankle-deep mud of the stickiest consist-ency imaginable. After a few yards Roz's wheels became im-movably jammed and she had to be *dragged* instead of rolled along. Following two miles of this hell we left the mud behind, as the track rose even more steeply—and now we were plough-ing our way through new snow a foot deep. Roz took a very dim view of it all; she thought we'd been through enough snow in Europe last winter without repeating the performance. And I agreed. Yet actually there isn't any comparison as far as temperatures are concerned. At 7 p.m. yesterday, 9,500 feet up in the Himalayas, I was literally dripping with sweat, though wearing only slacks and a shirt. Which just shows what last winter in Europe was like. (And which also shows the terrific exertion entailed in getting Roz up that damnable track.) By 5.45 p.m., when we were still stuck in the mud, it was dark— but I knew that an almost-full moon would soon rise from behind the mountains. For a moment, at that stage, I con-sidered returning to Shoja for the night. However, a built-in defect always defeats common sense on these occasions, by never allowing me to turn back, and before long I was suffering for my rashness.

During the next two and a half hours I struggled against the soft snow and the preposterous gradient—which was much more severe than that encountered on the far higher Babusar Pass— and by nine o'clock I had begun to feel really scared. Apart from the unbeatable hell of our June trek through the Indus Gorge this was the most frightening experience of my life. Since last winter's unfortunate encounter in Serbia, forest, snow and moonlight ring only one bell for me—*wolves*—and every time I heard a rustle I would have jumped a foot if I'd had the energy. I rapidly evolved the theory that Himalayan wolves are twice as big and ten times as fierce as the Yugoslav brand (which seems only logical) but happily there was no opportunity to prove this.

As we ascended the gradient became even crueller and the snow lay even thicker. I realized now that there was no chance of crossing the pass that night and several times I was tempted to ease the situation by abandoning Roz and searching alone for some dwelling. But here sentiment overcame reason; if we were going to be lost for ever in a snow-drift then it seemed fitting to me that we should be lost together. At this stage I was totally exhausted and had to stop every five or six yards, leaning my arms on Roz's handlebars and my head on my arms. Then I caught myself going to sleep in this position— which would have ended the story!—so for future pauses I just stood and gasped, while the sweat trickled down my face onto my bare arms. At every bend in the track I looked desperately for the outline of a rooftop in the moonlight—which was now very bright, as the clouds had scattered—and eventually I got to the point of fancying that big rocks were houses. Then, at last, a real rooftop did appear and instantly my resistance cracked. The house was only about forty yards away and dropping Roz on the track I crawled to the entrance, which was approached over a narrow plank 'bridge' laid from the edge of the track to the first floor balcony. (The ground floor of these farm-houses is always used for sheltering live-stock and storing fodder and grain.) Fumbling my way along the balcony I came to an open door and though no light was visible a child could be heard crying within. Being afraid of scaring the family by appearing too suddenly I called out '*Nemuste!*' But there was no response so I entered a pitch-dark room and then saw a faint flicker of firelight through a trap-door in the ceiling. Ascending a long, shaky ladder I put my head over the edge of the opening and rather timidly repeated—'*Nemuste!*' As I'd expected the unfortunate people were scared to bits—naturally enough, as even in summertime few foreigners travel through this region. Two young women screamed and jumped up from the central fireplace, which, as in Malana, was the room's only 'furniture'. They fled to a corner, each clutching an infant, as their husbands stood up and tried to look threatening, and an older man asked me in Hindi where I'd come from. I replied—'Kulu, with cycle,' and climbed the last rungs of the ladder into the warm room. Then, feeling too done in for any further explanations, I simply lay down by the fire and impolitely went fast asleep—as good a sample of sign-language as you could get!

On awakening ten hours later I found myself covered in a deliciously warm padded quilt and the fire was burning brightly and the two young women, reassured as to the intruder's harmlessness, were laughingly preparing chapattis and dal for my breakfast—God bless them! I discovered then that Roz had been rescued from the track and carefully put on the balcony for the night—and that her saddle-bag had been unstrapped and laid beside my head as I slept. This consideration touched me very much and was typical of the thoughtfulness I have experienced everywhere among allegedly uncouth peasants; obviously my host had reckoned that I might waken during the night and start to worry about my possessions.

This morning the sky was partly overcast again, but though it was snowing lightly the clouds were not low and there was no sign of the forecast blizzard which had been the cause of my ordeal. When I stepped out onto the balcony the view made me gasp with astonishment at the incredible climb we'd done through the darkness of the previous evening. I was looking down, down, down into the dark depths of a thickly forested valley and away to the north high Himalayan peaks were faintly reflecting the pale gold of the rising sun. Otherwise the colouring of the scene was subdued—grey sky, rocky crags, black forest—except where new snow had made the nearby pines, with their dainty, glittering burdens, look like gigantic Christmas trees.

From a practical point of view the new snow was less pleasing: we set out at 9.30 a.m. and it took us four and a half hours to cover the four miles to the top. The snow was always knee-deep and would have been difficult enough to battle through minus a bicycle. Of course I realized now that the Tibetans had left Roz out of the reckoning when they advised me so badly yesterday. Clearly they were thinking of carrying a load on the back: like sensible people they have never attempted to bring bicycles over mountain passes. However, after a good night's rest I thoroughly enjoyed the struggle: I was in no hurry and being alone amidst such surroundings is to me the quintessence of 'travellers' joy'. There was not a mark on the snow until we ploughed through it, not a movement but the slowly eddying flakes and a few swiftly swooping birds, not a sound but the soft plop of snow from branches to ground. Usually the trees were dense on either side but when I passed a break in their ranks tremendous, craggy peaks were visible, almost at eye-level, in the near distance. Towards mid-day the sky began so clear and by the time we had reached the pass the sun was thining from a blueness enhanced by streamers of wispy cloud.

From here the panoramas to north and south provided a remarkable contrast. Behind me the peaks were snow-laden and sharp and the valleys deep and dark: before me lay ridge after ridge of rounded mountains, their summits merely dusted with snow and the wide, shallow valleys between them warm with golden sunshine.

It was 2 p.m. when we started down—and in this context 'down' means a descent of 8,000 feet in twenty-three miles. Snow lay thick on the track for the first two miles and Roz and I more or less tobogganed over it together: it was an extraordinary sensation to be moving so effortlessly, after the violent exertion of the climb. Soon there was no more snow, except on odd shaded patches, yet because of the gruesome gradients and chaotically rough surface I had to walk about five of the next nine miles. By then we had descended—incredibly—to a mellow valley where huge orange trees were laden with ripe fruit. (I stopped at a tiny hamlet to buy a dozen luscious oranges for threepence.) Lemons the size of grapefruit also flourish here; when I first saw these monsters in the Kulu valley I thought that they *were* misshapen grapefruit and only discovered my mistake on buying one. This was a very 'Spanish' valley; apart from the orange-groves, at river-level, the bare mountain-sides were dotted with cacti and on the valley floor little fields of young wheat glistened like green silk.

I was able to freewheel down the next twelve miles—though the surface remained abominable—and we arrived at this camp on the banks of the Sutlej at 5.30 p.m. Fortunately there weren't many Tiblets to be examined so I'm going to bed early in preparation for to-morrow's crossing of the Narkanda Pass. This is only twenty-six miles away, but we are now a mere 2,600 feet above sea-level and Narkanda lies at 9,100 feet.

## TIBETAN ROAD-CAMP NEAR NARKANDA: 30 DECEMBER

By 8 a.m. we were on our way. For a few miles the road followed the Sutlej before joining that famous Hindustan–Tibet highway which, north of this point, has been closed to all civilian traffic since the Chinese invasion in October 1962. At the junction a new sign-post says 'Tibet 115 ms.', and here I dismounted to stand for a moment looking longingly up that road. What I would have given to be allowed to follow it! But perhaps some day I *will* get to Tibet, however ludicrous the idea may seem at the moment.

From the junction our road climbed very steeply for about five miles, till the Sutlej valley looked like an aerial view beneath us. Then the highway penetrated the heart of this range, winding round and round the arid flanks of grey-brown, treeless mountains. For fourteen miles the ascent was gradual, though continuous, and I was able to cycle most of the way—again in shirt-sleeves, under a cloudless sky. This would have been another most enjoyable trek but for the incessant heavy military traffic going towards Tibet: to see it one would think that a full-scale war was in progress on the frontier at this very moment. Countless truck-loads of unenthusiastic-looking young troops were interspersed with truck-loads of arms, ammunition,

pack-mules, fodder and general supplies. Watching these interminable convoys of mule-trucks and fodder-trucks I pitied
India's present military plight; there can be no more difficult
terrain in the world than the Hindustan–Tibet border area.

Because of its new strategic importance this road, which was
never designed for heavy traffic, is now being widened and improved at top speed—though that is hardly the *mot juste* for any
construction-work in this part of the world. It took us nearly
four hours to cover the fourteen 'cycleable' miles, so frequent
were the long delays caused by blasting operations. At each of
these halts Roz and I were on one side of the closed stretch of
road and the military convoys were queueing on the other side
—thus I inadvertently did my good deed for the day by providing the troops with an intriguing and much appreciated break
in the monotony of their journey. I myself was almost equally
intrigued by the activities of the road-workers—many of whom
were Indians on this sector. After a piece of jutting cliff had
been blasted away they swarmed over the road to move the
piles of shattered rock by hand—and if a chunk was too big to
be carried by two men then it had to be broken up with a
mallet. An impatient traveller in a hurry would soon go berserk
on this route.

Five miles from Narkanda we ran into more trouble. Here
the mountain was again wooded and, this being its northern
side, the road suddenly became a menacing mass of black ice.
Now we really *were* back where we had started from and as soon
as I saw the stuff I could most vividly visualize the road from
the ferry-berth at Dunkirk on 16 January 1963! I struggled on
over this glassy slide for about half a mile, but both Roz and
myself were continually losing our grip; with the road so narrow
and winding, and the traffic so heavy, and the drop beyond
the edge so horrific my nerve soon broke. Military assistance
seemed the solution and having waited some twenty minutes
we were rescued by an officers' snow-chained Land-Rover, en
route back to Simla; the officers had some rude things to say
about my sanity, especially when I declined their kind offer
of a lift all the way and insisted on being unloaded at Narkanda.

Despite the lower altitude it's very much colder on this treeless, windswept ridge than on the wooded Jalori Pass. This

camp is in a fairly sheltered spot, on the southern slope, yet it's still bitterly cold. There are about 300 adults here and sixty-two children, one of whom has pneumonia; I'm very much afraid he'll die during the night. This crisis puts me in a heartbreaking position, because his mother comes and kneels in front of me at intervals, touching my feet with her head and beseeching me to give him pills. She won't accept my repeated affirmations that I'm not a doctor, and at such moments I feel acutely frustrated by that inherent stupidity which prevents me from learning foreign languages; I would give anything to be able to talk to this woman.

Near the tent in which the boy is dying another, larger tent has been converted into a miniature temple and here five Lamas have assembled to read the *Bardo Thödol*. They are all charming men, with simple, open faces and gentle manners, and they received me most courteously when I explained through the interpreter that though I couldn't give the child any effective medicine I had come to pray for him—an action which, to my discomfort, reduced the mother to tears of gratitude. The usual elaborate *thankas* were decorating the sides of the tent and ancient, ceremonial vessels lay in rows before the Lamas. Unfortunately the eating of the dreaded (by me) *torma* was an inescapable part of the ritual: but having forced myself to swallow it I was able hastily to wash down the vile concoction with many cups of buttered tea.

This is the only camp where I've found the majority of children in very poor shape and where many adults desperately need medical care. The explanation of the adults' bad health and serious injuries must be overwork and the lifting of too heavy rocks—you can imagine the pressure put on road-workers all along this stretch of vital communication. The pleading, trustful way in which they come to show me their injuries would wring a tear from a stone; yet the adults, like the children, are so amenable to affection that if you put an arm round them, pat them on the head and talk kindly to them they immediately relax and beam happily, apparently forgetting their disappointment at not being miraculously cured. Such a lovable people—it saddens me beyond expression to think that this is my last night among them.

SIMLA: 31 DECEMBER

While I was having my breakfast of buttered tea and moo-moo the father of the sick child came to tell me that his son had died during the night; the mother was too grief-stricken to appear.

We had an easy forty-mile run from Narkanda to Simla. For most of the way the road ran level around mountain after mountain, giving me my best ever view of the Himalayas. What a spectacle! Hundreds of chunky, dazzling peaks stretch all along the horizon from Dharamsala in the west to as far as the eye can see in the east and the familiar peaks above the Nursery are seen from here to be the very beginning of the range—beyond them is only the bluish void of the plains. From these 16,000 footers the summits rise gradually to a triumphant climax of 23–25,000 footers, lorded over by Nanda Devi on the threshold of Tibet. Looking at this magnificent barricade one has an odd feeling that *nothing* lies beyond it, so overwhelming is the impression of achievement and finality.

Nearing Simla the road plunged steeply down, and on this descent we passed three recently crashed trucks which had skidded off at icy bends and gone hurtling over the precipice.

When we arrived here at 4 p.m. Pauline took one horrified look and then metaphorically picked me up with a pair of tongs and dropped me in the bathroom. I can't say I blame her, as my clothes hadn't been taken off for a fortnight and I've never in my life *felt* so filthy—which is saying something! By now I'm bathed and fine-combed and have been pronounced free of vermin and fit to accompany the Menteths to a New Year's Party.

As I sit writing my last diary-entry for 1963, and reflecting on my experiences in the past year, it's strange to think that when I left Ireland I was seeking only the satisfaction of adventure and discovery—but now, after spending the first half-year 'travelling hopefully', I have realized that it is far better 'to arrive'. Though at this moment I impatiently long to be home in Ireland I am determined to return to the Tibetans in 1965.

# Epilogue in Europe

On a cold, grey day at the end of March, five weeks after my return from India, I first met a Tibetan in Western surroundings. The setting was a London hotel lounge and the Tibetan was a young man of twenty-one who had just arrived from Switzerland, where he had been helping with a resettlement scheme since the previous December. I'm not sure what I had expected four months in Europe to do to a Tibetan but they seemed to have done no harm to Lobsang. He brought with him a calmness and dignity which I personally found very soothing at that time, suffering as I was from my first dose of concentrated publicity.

Now I could see for myself the famous Tibetan adaptability. This boy was superbly at ease, though at the same time one was aware of his essential 'differentness'. Unlike many Orientals met in Europe he was not striving to ape Western ways and attitudes but was simply accommodating himself to his new environment to the extent required by good manners.

After the discussion for which we had met I accompanied Lobsang to Waterloo, and it was on the Underground that he made me realize how quickly I had become reinfected by the feverish maelstrom of our Western civilization. As we descended the stairs a train could be heard approaching—whereupon everyone sprinted desperately down to the platform and leaped on board as though devils were following. Only one solitary figure was left behind—Lobsang, who crossed the platform at his usual pace and sedately entered the train a moment before the doors closed. Sitting opposite me he remarked with a slight smile, 'It is not necessary to get worried and run to these trains. I have seen that if one goes away another comes very soon.'

Before we said good-bye that evening we had arranged that Lobsang should spend his summer holiday in Ireland.

N

Lobsang was the second youngest of a family of eight and both his parents died in 1945. To quote his own words, 'My mother died when my youngest brother was born and my father died six weeks later because he was so sad.' This cause of death being accepted as something entirely understandable reminded me once again of the strange fate of Sonam Nobo's mother at Dharamsala.

Lobsang's father had been a government official in Lhasa and in addition to his Civil Service duties—or possibly as part of them—he practised as an oracle. This information was given me in matter-of-fact tones as we crossed St James's Park, where the idea of anyone's father having been an oracle struck a delightfully exotic note. Yet this reference to an occupation so remote from our world highlighted those barriers which always divide East from West, however easy the *rapport* between individuals.

At the age of four Lobsang was adopted by his father's brother, an Incarnate Lama of the Gelugpas who was then Abbot of Tubung Churbu Monastery, twenty miles west of Lhasa. This small community of a hundred monks was one of two monasteries which the Abbot had founded, and here Lobsang spent his school holidays. His childhood was secure and contented, despite the rigorous *régime* traditional to Tibetan schools, where a pupil's powers of concentration are developed to the highest degree and the minimum of recreation is allowed. One of his aunts, who lived in Lhasa, was especially kind to him, and though his uncle was a very austere man, with whom it was impossible to have an informally relaxed relationship, Lobsang knew that he could rely on the Abbot's constant affection.

When the Lhasa uprising began on 17 March 1959, Lobsang at once fled to Tubung Churbu. Already his only sister—a pioneer of agricultural improvement—had been murdered by the Chinese and the family was sufficiently prominent for each member to be in grave danger at that time. In the Monastery preparations were being made for an escape to India, and two weeks later the Abbot set out with twenty-five followers—including Lobsang—and a train of sixty mules. Many of these pack-animals carried priceless loads, for the Abbot was intent on saving his library of ancient Sanskrit manuscripts and his famous collection of Thankas. As the main routes to the frontier were then being vigilantly patrolled by the Chinese all refugee caravans had to use unfrequented tracks over high passes and this comparatively short journey—during which half the mules were lost through injury—took more than three gruelling months.

The first man who heads for the moon will have a much clearer picture of what to expect on arrival than Lobsang had en route to India. In the course of this trek he suffered acutely from loneliness and often wept at leaving behind him his brothers, his friends and his country. As yet he had no conception of what it meant to be a refugee and his imagination could not begin to visualize the sort of world towards which he was travelling. In Tibet he had never known the significance of money; his needs had always been provided for and the idea of earning was completely foreign to him—but soon he was to be alone in an environment where money is the determining factor in most people's lives.

When the caravan at last reached Kalimpong the Abbot retired to a local monastery to recover from an illness brought on by his ordeal and Lobsang lodged for three months in the home of Sherpa Tenzing of Everest. Most of the Abbot's retainers now dispersed to fend for themselves, but those who were too old or infirm to do so are still with him in Benares, where for the past few years he has held the chair of Sanskrit Studies at the famous Hindu University. Fortunately most of his manuscripts and all the Thankas survived the journey, and these latter were one of the chief attractions at an International Exhibition of Oriental Art held recently in Delhi.

At this stage Lobsang spoke only Tibetan and some Chinese, so his months in Kalimpong were spent studying Hindi, Nepali and English. Then he decided to find a job which would make him financially independent, while enabling him to perfect his English, and a few weeks later he had become house-boy to an American family in New Delhi.

In our society this would not seem very remarkable but in the East such a step required considerable strength of character from a young man who had been accustomed to three personal servants and had never been allowed to put on his own boots. In some refugee circles Lobsang now found himself regarded as a fool; with his connections he could have lived comfortably in idleness. But to him this would have been infinitely more degrading than working as a servant and, apart from his desire to be independent, he also wished to equip himself with some means of helping the thousands of his illiterate fellow-country-men who were then drifting about Northern India in bewildered misery. Realizing their difficulties he felt that a core of educated, English-speaking Tibetans could achieve a great deal by acting as liaison officers between them and the Twentieth Century.

Lobsang's employers were kind and appreciative but as a house-boy he found himself with insufficient time for serious study, so after nine months he left the Americans—despite their offer to double his wages—and went as a voluntary worker to Mrs Bedi's School for Young Lamas. A few months later Miss Joyce Pearce, of Ockenden Venture, visited this school, met Lobsang and offered him the opportunity to study in England.

For the next six months, while the necessary formalities were being completed, Lobsang worked as an assistant secretary in His Holiness's office at Dharamsala. Curiously enough we never met there, though our terms overlapped by three months, but we had many mutual friends in the area—and a few mutual enemies, despite Lobsang's reluctance to acknowledge any man as an enemy!

On the day of Lobsang's arrival in Ireland flights to Cork were delayed by fog and I asked an official at the bus terminus to contact my hotel when Mr Lobsang arrived. In due course the telephone rang and a voice in rich Cork brogue asked, 'Is that Miss Murphy? Well, I've got a Tie-bet-an here and I'm keeping him for you to take—would that be right?' I replied gravely that it would indeed; the implication that a Tie-bet-an was a species of dangerous wild animal made me feel that I had been cast in the rôle of a qualified circus-trainer. Yet when I arrived at the terminus fifteen minutes later Lobsang and the official were deep in conversation, and as we left the building the Cork man whispered to me, 'Gorr, he's a terrible nice little fella after all—real polite and friendly-like—good luck to ye!'

Two days later we left Lismore to hitch-hike to Galway, en route for the Aran Islands. Lobsang was an ideal travelling companion, so indifferent to what most Europeans would regard as discomfort that after a five-mile walk through pouring rain he still looked cheerful. Also he took it for granted that everything must be accomplished on a shoe-string and this, when one belongs to a society in which all one's friends have considerably more money than oneself, makes a welcome change.

I had been looking forward to a return to Inishere—the smallest of the three Arans—during all my time abroad. The way of life on this little island is as primitive as one could find anywhere in Europe. The only roads are rough dirt tracks, the traffic consists entirely of donkeys, water is drawn from wells, clothes are home-spun, Irish is the spoken language, and apart from vegetables, milk, eggs and fish all supplies must come out from the mainland. There may seem to be little affinity between landlocked Tibet and an isle in the Atlantic, yet I had felt—and Lobsang soon confirmed this feeling—that a Tibetan would find himself at home on Inishere.

The two and a half hour journey from Galway was Lobsang's longest sea voyage, but luckily it was calm and when we anchored off the South Island a small fleet of currachs—frail craft of wood-lathe and tarred canvas—immediately surrounded us to ferry passengers and goods ashore.

The island was looking its loveliest on this cloudless August morning, with the sharp Atlantic light heightening the contrast between silver sands and vivid little fields. On the strand sturdy donkeys queued to take sacks of coal, flour and sugar to the two tiny shops, and the community's only mule-cart—a recent innovation—stood by to bring the mail to the Post Office. So still is the island on such a day that the rattle of the anchor-chain sounded almost aggressive, and so easily do the islanders move about their tasks that my own impatience to board a currach suddenly appeared ridiculous.

Boat-days are something of an event and a vast crowd of twenty or thirty people, plus three or four dogs, usually assemble to welcome the *Naomh Eanna*. Inevitably Lobsang's arrival

created a sensation and I couldn't help feeling embarrassed at
the uninhibited curiosity with which he was regarded. But I
needn't have worried; it transpired afterwards that he had
observed a family party weeping as they said good-bye to an
emigrant daughter and with refugee understanding he had been
much more aware of this pathetically permanent feature of
island life than of his own conspicuousness.

During the next few weeks we shared a friend's rented cottage, washed at the well three-quarters of a mile away, slept
flea-bagged on the floor and played Mah Jong by candlelight
—and Lobsang obviously revelled in this escape from the suave-
ness of Europe to the sternness of Aran. He enthusiastically
appropriated many of the daily chores and within hours of our
arrival had dug a very splendid Asian-type latrine, while his
zeal for fetching water soon earned him the nick-name of
'Choo-Lin'—'Water-Carrier'. He was no less zealous to collect
dung for the fire, but here slight complications arose; some
cow-pats contained insects and were therefore not considered
eligible, by a Buddhist, for burning. Similarly, forays to pick
barnacles and periwinkles were quietly avoided.

Another aspect of Buddhism was revealed by Lobsang's dealings with the Islanders, some of whom are not conspicuously
friendly, even to visitors from the mainland. At first Lobsang
found one of the men downright insulting. On the day after
our arrival he returned from the village looking somewhat dis-
concerted and, telling me of this encounter, concluded, 'I was
very angry, but my uncle taught me never to seem angry, even
if I can't help feeling it, so I said nothing. Perhaps if I keep
nice to him he will become nice to me. He can't help being
ignorant of outside things and having these terrible manners.'
A few days later I met the man concerned and to my astonishment he was extravagant in his admiration for Lobsang and
was most sympathetic towards Tibet, a country of which he had
never previously heard. And when we left Inishere three weeks
later—by which time Lobsang had become a universal favourite
—the 'Tie-bet-an' was presented by this man with a farewell gift.

In conversation with Lobsang I often became uncomfortably
aware of the crudeness of my own attitudes and reactions. We
frequently discussed the general Tibetan problem and the

personalities we both knew in India, and as time passed I noticed that my tendency to make harsh criticisms was being curbed by Lobsang's disinclination to impute evil to anyone. He managed to assess all types of people astutely, without ever being malicious, and if an individual's misbehaviour was too blatant to be ignored he would, without condoning it, refer to some extenuating factor which should be taken into account before judgement was passed. Nor was this merely *esprit de corps*; he showed equal charity towards non-Tibetans—except when vigorously denouncing what appeared to him to be the barbarically low standard of Western sexual morality.

Yet Lobsang was no devitalized prig, and I suspect that he followed his uncle's precepts only when they were acceptable to him personally. With a mischievous gleam in the eye he told me about the elaborate Tibetan carpet, woven in his parents' home, which he had brought to Switzerland. His uncle had instructed him never to part with this treasure, but as Lobsang wanted a transistor radio and as the Abbot had confiscated the one he bought in India—'Because it distracts the boy from his studies'—Lobsang promptly sold his carpet and acquired a *de luxe* short-wave set on which he can get All-India Radio and Radio Peking. This transistor was of course brought to Inishere but Lobsang obviously realized that the object of the expedition was to escape such irritations, and we only learned afterwards that it had been used regularly in the small hours of the morning.

In the evenings, after supper, we used to sit around the open fire and return to Tibet with Lobsang. 'Choo-Lin' had seen far more of his own country than do most Tibetans, for at the age of fifteen he was taken by his uncle on an eighteen months' journey to a sacred mountain in West Tibet. This pilgrimage of a Very High Lama to a Very Sacred Mountain was obviously a major operation. The caravan consisted of 100 horses and mules and 300 yaks, carrying camping equipment and stores for sixty monks and servants. The desolate nature of the country in West Tibet made it necessary to carry this vast quantity of food, and Lobsang's reference to sacks of dried meat and compressed vegetables reminded me that our dehydrated foods are not, after all, unique.

At nightfall, during this trek, everyone except the Abbot helped set up camp and Lobsang remarked that this was excellent training for him and his young companions. Occasionally there was some excitement—when a panther killed a dog or hundreds of wild horses were sighted galloping across the steppes. Quite often dangerously flooded rivers had to be negotiated and then the mules and horses swam with their riders through the swift, icy water and the yaks were ferried on square, flat-bottomed boats of wood and yak-hide. But on the whole this sounded a happy and peaceful journey, and Lobsang looks back on that period with inevitable nostalgia, realizing that his Tibet has by now been changed for ever.

At that time Tubung Churbu employed three traders who travelled regularly between Lhasa, India, China and Mongolia. The Monastery also had its own 'Civil Service', and a group of these officials annually toured the countryside to collect the dzo-butter tax. It was soon after returning from the pilgrimage, and shortly before the Uprising, that Lobsang was appointed to one such group which, in the course of its tour, encountered a battalion of Chinese soldiers. As the Chinese were then feeling daily more insecure they refused to accept the leader's explanation of his business and captured all but two of the party. On the following night, while the guards were being distracted by an attempted escape from another of the prison tents, Lobsang managed to break out from his tent, seize a horse and flee towards Lhasa. For ten days he rode alone, avoiding the Chinese-infested main road, sleeping out in freezing temperatures and living on a few handfuls of tsampa: but he says that the loneliness and the fear of recapture were even worse than the cold and hunger. When he finally reached Tubung Churbu he collapsed and was ill for six weeks. A month or so after his recovery the Uprising took place and he never heard what happened to the other members of the group.

I found that forming a friendship with an individual refugee helped me to understand certain aspects of the general problem which I had not fully grasped while working at Dharamsala.

Lobsang's conversation emphasized the fact that most people depend, perhaps more than they realize, on the stability of that material and moral environment which gives shape and signifi-

cance to individual lives. Even when families leave their home-
land for years at a stretch the consciousness that they belong
there in a special sense, and can return in time to their own
niche, makes for security and self-assurance. Therefore the
sudden violent dispossession accompanying a refugee flight is
much more than the loss of a permanent home and a traditional
occupation, or than the parting from close friends and familiar
places. It is also the death of the person one has become in a
particular context, and every refugee must be his or her own
midwife at the painful process of rebirth.

# *Appendix I*

*Letter from Judy Pullen, volunteer with Canadian University Service Overseas.*

Kangra Boys' School
3 July 1964.

Dear Dervla,

I was so thrilled to get your letter in March—we'd been wondering about you since the day you rode away for Kulu.

Lois was really sick for two months in Delhi with amœbic hepatitis, giardia and another virus infection. The poor kid went through hell—at one time it looked as though she'd have to be sent home to Canada. However, she recovered and returned to us—we have yet to see how wise that was because she's not in top health yet.

Our C.U.S.O. Conference in Bombay in March was great fun. I also went to Pach Marhi for two days—heartwarming reunion with 250 of our precious Kangra family. Got back to Kangra to find the Lama School had moved up to the cooler climate of Lower Dharamsala—a much healthier spot for them, surrounded by lovely gardens and vegetable fields they planted themselves. But I was really unhappy to lose those studious afternoons in their classroom.

And then the *big blow*—with only two days' warning our beloved Rimpoche was called to a new job in Delhi. You can't imagine how stunned and unhappy we were. The kids cried and wailed so hard on his last night that the Indians thought half our school had died.

A pretty desolate time followed until Lois arrived back unexpectedly one day. We cooked all our own food but I'm afraid she didn't keep that up for long. The weather was as hot as heck and there was no water supply at the school except for an hour morning and night. We walked one and a half miles to the river every day and made the kids wash themselves and their clothes.

Then Mr Kundeling asked me to move to Dharamsala to

continue teaching the Lamas. You can't imagine how torn my loyalties were! My teaching with the children was getting pretty frustrating with the rapid turnover and I was finding it harder and harder to keep my patience in class—'This is *my* nose, that is *your* nose' routine. Lois was terrific—she was really firm about me going if I wanted to make any real contribution with my teaching. I felt miserable as I said good-bye to the kids and cried the whole way up in the bus as I looked back over those seven crazy, wonderful months in that old building. But as soon as I got off the bus and was greeted by dozens of grinning and friendly children I felt much better.

The work here has surpassed all expectations. In addition to two English classes, I'm giving lectures in geography, general science, hygiene, current events, world history, etc. It all sounds very grand but I'm just trying to give some grounding in each subject. A special translator was brought from Delhi so I lecture in English and he translates as I go. The atmosphere became charged with excitement as they learned about the solar system, changes of season, etc. Late into the evening monks could be seen clustered around the globe with flashlights and little balls trying to work out lunar and solar eclipses. They're just lapping everything up and it's such a joy to teach such interested pupils. Zimey Rimpoche, the head Lama and principal, is young, charming and brilliant. He keeps me running to my books with his intelligent questions on satellites, sound-waves, splitting the atom, etc. Who said Tibetans were resistant to Western science and learning? I spend hours curled up on a rug in his room— speaking Tibetan and English and teaching him but, best of all, learning from one of the most learned Tibetan scholars in India!

On Saturday mornings I climb up to the Dance-Drama School where I'm teaching modern dance exercises to the girls. I don't know who was stiffer after the first lesson—them or me! The girls have improved a lot—they really had no idea how to exercise and develop flexibility and strong backs. Oliver says they all complain of back-aches—maybe we can fix that! Anyway it's a wonderful chance for me to learn their dances and songs.

I go home to Kangra once or twice a week to spend the night

and help Lois. I really look forward to those visits because I miss the children dreadfully. Those Kangra nights are usually sleepless ones—if we aren't battling bed-bugs or rats it's the heat or a storm that keeps us awake. But it's well worth it.

My first night at the Lama School was a bit of a nightmare. I didn't get to bed till about 1 a.m. after the streams of visitors finally left. Then I started having terrible dysentery pains that got worse and worse. The climax came when something dropped off the shelf onto my head—a large, ugly rat! Soon I had five huge monsters rushing about my room—I had to leave the light on all night and keep kicking them off the bed. I've never seen such bold monsters! At 5 a.m. a Lama came to sweep my room. I remember wondering if they thought they were going to sweep at that unearthly hour every day—but I've never been so happy to see a human face after that nightmare with the rats! The rest of the day passed in a haze of pain as monks rushed to and fro to nurse me. Then a jeep came in the late afternoon and took me up to Juliet's little bungalow where I stayed for four days to recover.

Then, five weeks ago now, I got sick again but stayed home at the Lama School where I was smothered with loving attention. At one point, when I had a fever, there were five monks standing in a circle around my bed fanning me with newspapers. The head Lama and two other Rimpoches were amongst them. They practically blew me off the bed in their enthusiasm but we had a good laugh over it. When I seemed to be getting sicker after five days, Rimpoche insisted on calling Juliet. I was vomiting all my meals by this time and feeling very dizzy. Mr Kundeling came with his jeep and I felt a fool as they took me back to Juliet's. And so began a dandy bout of jaundice and infectious hepatitis. I stayed with Juliet till 21 June and then came down here to Dr Haslem. She says it will be another week before I can go back. You can't imagine how frustrated and fed-up I am at losing so much precious time.

Juliet was a dear—nothing was too much trouble for her and she took wonderful care of me.

And God bless Oliver! He was such a crazy dear—kept me laughing instead of crying. Claudia (Oliver's fiancée) arrived ten days before the wedding and she couldn't be better suited for Oliver—a good head on her shoulders, modest, sweet and full of fun. We got along famously. Dierdre and a friend arrived for the wedding. The rehearsal the night before had me in fits of laughter. Everything was in a shambles because Stuart Menteth didn't come and Thomas (Oliver's best friend from Switzerland) didn't come. Finally, Mr Kundeling was asked to give away the bride and his interpreter, Rinzin, was best man. But neither they nor the bride and groom knew the Anglican wedding service. It was 10 p.m., Friday, before Juliet finally hounded Oliver into getting Rinzin and she went through the whole service for them. Oliver concentrated very hard but got hopelessly muddled and had us all in an uproar.

They had a gorgeous day for the wedding—I was determined to go. The little church looked lovely and was filled with Tibetan, Indian and Western friends. Claudia looked sweet in a white and silver sari—Dierdre in a pink one—Mr Kundeling and Rinzin in full Tibetan dress with high boots—what a scene! The service went very well considering English wasn't the native tongue of any of those involved—including the Indian minister. Oliver repeated his vows with such intensity and volume that I nearly fell off my seat!

The luncheon at Dall Lake was a feast like I've never seen before—Chumba did a superb job. Your telegram gave us all a thrill. The Nursery children danced, we had a lovely tea at four o'clock and then everyone left.

Finally Claudia and Oliver set off on their one and a half day honeymoon up to Daramkote—Claudia on a horse and Oliver walking beside with a huge pack on his back—they looked adorable.

Lois is now living in Upper Dharamsala in what used to be the Education Department. The house was quickly vacated three weeks ago and Lois went there to receive 120 kids who arrived nearly dead. She, Oliver, Claudia, Juliet and Doris battled long into the night to save their lives. Those kids had camped four months on the border without shelter, food or help. They buried two of their number there and then permission came to enter India—on grounds of compassion. Seventeen were left in a nearby hospital—nearly dead—and the others came on here on a nightmare of a train ride in the most

o

blistering heat. You wouldn't believe it unless you saw it—
they're still only shells and skeletons of children. Two more have
died—one in Lois' arms on a frantic jeep-ride to Kangra—of
worm-convulsions. Lois had to cremate the body herself. And
now they're having emotional fits, hysterics and an attempted
suicide—it's so criminal I can't believe it's true. And we've had
three tragic deaths in our Kangra family in the past four days
—this blistering heat in Kangra is taking its toll. Life is a bit
of a nightmare now. But I'm still madly in love with my
Tibetans and don't see how I'll leave in September.

Love, Judy.

Upper Dharamsala<br>4 September 1964

Dear Dervla,
    Lois cracked up again about three weeks ago and spent ten
days at the Mission Hospital. It was the same old liver trouble
and I am quite worried because it bothers her constantly
though she's back on the job again. It's a miracle she lasted this
long after the terrific strain she's been under since early June
when those very sick kids arrived. It was a long, hard struggle
but she lost only two of them, and even the most seriously disturbed children are now normal, healthy and delightful Tibetan
kids. By now they are such a boisterous and energetic crew that
they quite wear Lois out. Since their health improved, however,
she has time to enjoy them and goes for long walks all over
the mountain-side with them. When Lois was away sick I spent
the week-end there. One of the three T.B. girls (sleeping in
Lois' bedroom because there is no other place) developed
pneumonia and was a pretty miserable little tyke. I took all
three of them over to the Nursery where Thomas (who has
replaced Oliver) put them in a separate room. I was just getting
ready to dash back down here to teach on Monday morning
when His Holiness strode into the school on a surprise visit.
We were all terribly thrilled. I dashed down here after he left
and was in the middle of teaching my morning class when the
door curtain was swept aside and in strode His Holiness again.
I don't know who was more shocked—he or I! He stayed at
the back and watched me teach for five minutes—I was a little

heap of nervous jelly by the time he left. He'd even spoken to me in English when he first came in. Both his Senior and Junior Tutors came to lecture to our students on different afternoons.

I sat in on both lectures and was pleased at how much I understood. The Junior Tutor is a particularly wonderful person—I was most impressed by him. He seems so wise and kind and compassionate—I had a wonderful talk with him after but got stumped a couple of times when he used high honorific words that I'd never heard before. All the Lamas have the highest and most devoted regard for him—as many as 5,000 people at a time used to sit for six hours on end in Lhasa to listen to his sermons. He certainly had me spellbound when he spoke though I couldn't follow everything he said.

Lois and I have decided to stay for another year and a half—I couldn't possibly leave now with all there is to do. I'm trying to write a series of English–Tibetan readers to be used in the schools—all the Indian ones are hopeless. Now that I'm quite fluent in Tibetan and familiar with the situation and the people, it would be a waste to throw it all over and pull out now when I might be able to make a concrete contribution in Tibetan education. Besides, I absolutely adore all these people and don't see how I could say good-bye. My work is so exciting and challenging that it doesn't even seem like work. Lois feels the same and will probably stay on as long as I do. She's terribly excited at the prospect of perhaps helping a Doctor who hopes to come here next spring and set up a school in Macleod Ganj where she can train Tibetan nurses.

And now for the Nursery situation. Lois and I have seen a lot of Pema (younger sister of His Holiness, who has replaced Mrs Tsiring Dolma) and the more we see her the more we like her. She's a wonderful gal and is working like a dog at the Nursery. She's there from 9 a.m. to 8 p.m. seven days a week. She was sick with tonsillitis one week and Thomas ordered her to bed but she refused to go and came to work every day. Everyone is just thrilled with her, and things at the Nursery have improved 100% since she and Miss Betts have come. Miss Betts (who has come from Simla to replace Juliet) thinks the world of Pema. Thomas is happy with both of them. The two lovely new white Tibetan buildings, above Juliet's house, have both been given over for the new Dispensary. Thomas will have a beautiful big room for himself, a lab., examination room and lots of room for sick children. Tibetans built the houses and did all the labour. The children should be moving in soon, but unfortunately Thomas has already fallen victim to hepatitis and has been down in the Kangra Mission Hospital for a week now.

Miss Betts is interested in training the staff and she's organized staff-lectures, etc. They had a staff party last week-end that was a huge success. Things have improved so much that Doris has decided to stay for at least another year. She feels that things are really moving at the Nursery now and Lois says Pema thinks the world of Doris and her hard and devoted work for the children. It's enough to restore your faith in human nature to see the team-work and friendship and co-operation in that Nursery now. Everyone's pulling *together* and with luck the Dharamsala Nursery will soon be a credit to all those concerned.

Pema just turned twenty-three this summer (by our years) so I'd say that she deserves a lot of credit for the way she's shouldered this responsibility so willingly and cheerfully. You can rest assured that the Nursery is in good hands.

Love from Judy.

# Appendix II

*Extract from 1965 Diary, written en route to a Tibetan Refugee camp in Nepal.*

## Dharamsala, 23 April 1965

When the bus from Patancot reached Lower Dharamsala at 12.40 p.m. I at once took the short cut to the Nursery—and never have I done that climb so quickly. I dashed through Forsythe Bazaar (noticing how many more Tibetans are there now, from Nepal) and I was scrambling up the steep path through the forest when I heard shouts of 'Amela!' and saw two Tiblets rushing through the trees with arms outstretched. What a welcome! I would not have known either of them and thought it rather remarkable that they recognized me. On reaching the camp several ayahs greeted me, and we were hugging each other joyfully when a sturdy little object came hurtling across the compound wearing an ear-to-ear grin: I had no difficulty in recognizing *this* Tiblet as Cama Yishy flung himself at me. When looking forward to our reunion I had thought it unlikely that he would remember 'Amela', much less display such enthusiastic affection, and I was so surprised by this demonstration that I promptly burst into tears—a re-action which annoyed me but which the ayahs took completely for granted.

It is hard to believe that the miserable children among whom I worked less than a year and a half ago have been transformed into these bouncing, bright-eyed, rosy-cheeked Tiblets. Had I been dropped into the compound by helicopter I would never have recognized the place; there are now twice the number of buildings—and half the number of children. The Swiss Red Cross has provided a nurse to work with Doris Betts (the S.C.F. nurse succeeding Juliet, who has been transferred to Simla and is engaged to a most likeable and talented Indian army officer), and Doris Murray is at last free to concentrate on the educational needs of the camp. Some of the children who were here in 1963 have returned to their parents and others have been transferred to Dalhousie, Mussoorie or Simla; the present policy is to keep numbers down to a maximum of 500, and Pema-la very wisely refuses to admit any but orphans from the road-camps.

Soon after my arrival I went to the upper nursery to pay my respects to Pema-la, His Holiness's younger sister, who has brought about this wonderful improvement. One feels that the future of the Tibetan community in exile depends largely on the leadership of the younger generation of educated Tibetans, and to know that there are people like Pema-la and Lobsang among them is tremendously encouraging.

I spent most of the afternoon playing with the Tiblets in the lower nursery. Cama Yishy has become very dictatorial, and Pema-la tells me that he is now leader of his age-group at prayers, dancing and lessons. If anything his charm has in-creased, but unlike the old days he is very possessive towards me. This afternoon he wanted me all to himself and tried to drive the others away, so I had to be tough and make him realize that I wanted to cuddle *the lot*—a situation which he accepted philosophically enough providing no one else sat on my right, where he well remembered he had long since staked his claim. It's priceless to see him putting my arm around himself so that my hand is where he likes it on his chest, and grinning triumphantly up at me, obviously conscious of having me where he wants me in every sense—he's a cunning little devil!

Today's most remarkable feat of recognition was achieved by Pooh-Bah. He was only three when last we met, yet he knew me at once and almost exploded with gurgles of joy in my arms. What a change there! He has become much more extrovert and sociable and has lost some of his good looks and all his diseases—which latter deprivation he must feel acutely, he so loved complaining.

Dharamsala: 24 April 1965

I could hardly sleep last night, I felt so excited and happy about the camp's transformation. And this morning provided another pleasant surprise when I had an audience with His

Holiness and found him much more relaxed and approachable than during our last meeting sixteen months ago. He seems to have matured a great deal in that brief time and to have gained in self-assurance, as though he has at last been able to come to terms with his strange situation. The impression I had today was of an astute young statesman in the making—yet when we came to touch on religion he spoke with an easy sincerity that was immensely moving and quite unlike his tense, watchful manner at our previous meeting. He looks considerably older now, and a little thinner—but very much happier.

This time I was not received formally in the audience chamber but was led to the verandah where His Holiness was sitting stroking a magnificent Lhasa Apso terrier with a long, silky, pale silver coat. He at once remarked how much weight I had lost and then went on to ask when I left Ireland. On hearing that I had been in London since 3 April he astonished me by observing 'so you were not at home to vote in the General Election on the 7th of April'. I wonder how many people outside Ireland are aware that we even had a General Election!

His Holiness's English has improved so much that nothing I said had to be translated—though he always spoke to me through his interpreter—and we had a long discussion on current Tibetan difficulties, particularly those with which I will soon be battling in Nepal. Some of his comments revealed a mischievous sense of humour which might not be fully appreciated by the senior lamas but which proved that he has no illusions about the extent to which some Tibetans worsen the refugee situation and that he does not wish to present to foreigners any false image of the Tibetan way of life. I could not but notice the temperamental affinity between himself and Pema-la (who has always been his closest friend) and I left the Palace feeling that the combined efforts of these two young people could eventually solve quite a number of problems.

# Index